Christ's

Humanity

A Thing

To Be Grasped

He did not think existing in the form of
and being equal to God as something to be grasped,
but emptied Himself taking the form of a slave.

By

Thomas G. Thompson

Published By:

Son Publishing

P.O. Box 793

Frazier Park, California 93225

christshumanity.com

ISBN 978 0 9851403 0 4

All Scripture texts are quoted from the English translations, of the New American Standard Bible or the Authorized King James Version, unless indicated otherwise. Throughout the book citations have been given without distinction or indication.

DEDICATION

My wife, Susan, wished not to be the focus of my dedication of this work and suggested we dedicate this labor of love directly to Jesus. The words herein we offer as an act of our deepest devotion and thanks to our Savior and Friend for all He has done and all He has promised to do. Jesus, all you want is our love and respect. It seems hardly enough, but then we could never out-give you. Come quickly, King Jesus. You are desperately needed here. We trust this book pleases you and that you can use it for your purposes.

All our love,

Thomas and Susan

ACKNOWLEDGMENTS

Without the help of two brave Spirit filled souls and brothers in the Lord this work would not have gone forward or reached completion, our God of grace will reward these saints for their faithfulness.

Without the help of my friend Bob Jaffray any reader coming from academia would not have read past the first chapter before closing the book. He made sense of what I had written and arranged it in an understandable order, and he kept me focused on the main point of the book. His skills made clear many difficult areas of thought. Bob and I met at least once a week for most of the process.

Wesley Searcy was a continual source of encouragement over and against the formidable odds of this work ever going to press. He did this against inevitable personal criticism. Constantly he reminded me of the opposing position almost at every turn. Among his ideas came the title Christ's Humanity-A Thing to be Grasped- a play on words because of what Jesus did not consider was a thing for Himself as something to be grasped.

The Holy Spirit Who was my constant companion through this glorious work and who kept reminding me it was His responsibility to show us the things of Christ. He influenced me from the original thought through all of the opposition, the research, selecting the right team, and supervising us all the way to the finish line. Thank you dear Spirit for your patience in leading us, the Father and the Son I am sure are eternally thankful as well. Amen.

TABLE OF CONTENTS

In this book we want to show that we must interpret the life experiences of Christ in terms of his humanity, and not his deity.

Consistent with sound orthodox teaching but without theological speculation, the truth as revealed in the Scripture concerning the humanity of Jesus Christ will be interpreted according to the literal hermeneutic in each of the following chapters, to the end that Christ will be known and appreciated as God but also a real man.

True believers hold that there is one and only one God, so references to the Father, Son and Holy Spirit as God must be explained. They must neither be understood as referring to more than one God, nor be understood to be merely different names for the one God or merely names for different ways the one God acts. The truth of there being one God in three inherent and eternal distinctions is called the Trinity.

Christ the Son of God of the Trinity became man as the God-Man, both fully God and fully man indissolubly joined in one, not temporarily but permanently forever. His becoming wholly man as well as God is called the incarnation. This is Jesus of the Bible. Jesus could be both fully God and fully man without ever coming in a state of humiliation but didn't. Rather, for the salvation of sinners He humbled Himself. But as the God-Man in his state of exaltation Jesus does now have divine authority and can freely use his inherent divine powers.

3. THE BIBLICAL DOCTRINE 45

Because we recognize Jesus as the Son of God we naturally tend to attribute things that He did to his divine abilities, rather than attributing them as Scriptures does to the Holy Spirit. Scripture is very clear in teaching that Christ acted by the power of the Holy Spirit.

4. REASONABLE QUESTIONS 66

But now when we consider who Jesus really was according to Scripture, we see that the various events can indeed be explained according to the biblical doctrine without calling on his divine abilities. This answers many reasonable questions that would otherwise naturally arise.

5. CHRIST'S HUMILIATION AND EXALTATION 82

In order for Christ, the incarnate Son of God, to be completely obedient to his Father He laid aside the use of his divine powers. The kenosis stated in Philippians Chapter 2 gives the biblical reason why Jesus did not depend on his inherent divine abilities in his state of humiliation.

After Jesus accomplished the redemption of sinners by his life and sacrifices in complete obedience to God his Father, He was exalted as the God-Man in his state of exaltation. He then assumed his position at the right hand of his Father and is presently at work in the second phase of his office of mediator. Now though still obedient to his Father, He is no longer limited to the use of only his human abilities.

6. CHRIST AS PROPHET 104

On the basis of Old Testament teaching and prophecies, Jesus as a human prophet by inspiration of the Holy Spirit could prophesy more details with regard to the fulfillment of previous prophecies. So these additional details in themselves do not necessarily indicate personal use of divine abilities. And as the Great Prophet that Scripture forecasts that would follow Moses, He could give new prophetic revelation.

Without the biblical doctrine of Christ's humanity, Christ could not have redeemed men from sin. So the doctrine of Christ's atonement and the biblical doctrine of Chapters 3 through 5 must be in harmony.

Without the biblical doctrine, Christians cannot take Christ's example seriously for their own personal sanctification. Moreover their future eschatological hope depends on the truth of the biblical doctrine of Chapters 3 through 5.

What we earnestly desire is for believers to be uplifted by a more full and true understanding of Christ's humanity.

APPENDICES

PREFACE

The greatest gift from God to mankind in addition to life itself is without a doubt his one and only begotten Son, the Lord Jesus Christ. God the Father actually did give us his eternally beloved Son and in order to restore all things to Himself did put Him in harm's way. However, without God's gift of the Holy Bible to define for us, and the Holy Spirit to illumine for us, who Christ is in his person, we would never appreciate just who He is or why God sent him; or for that matter, how Jesus was able to accomplish all that was expected from Him. Our understanding of his person and work, and the reason He came are necessary for our very salvation. Obviously the world, even with the Bible, is still unable to understand or appreciate Him for whom He is, or even to their own destruction appreciate why He was here.

But the real reason for this book is to reintroduce Him more accurately to those who already know Him, and to correct within the community of believers some false impressions of Him; false impressions currently accepted and taught within Christ's own body of believers. Church leaders and theologians worldwide have elected to believe and teach a wrong premise delineating the work of Christ, which affects the correct perception of his whole being.

The corner of the building is off plumb, and eventually it will show enough to require a necessary correction. In the truth concerning the person of the Lord Jesus Christ and the way he lived on earth, I see the building leaning noticeably. It affects one's daily walk in the Spirit and the intimate relationship with Jesus we long for.

But no one, who really loves him, would have intentionally misrepresented who He is or teach others to do so. However, it is easy enough to accept what appears to be a minor misinterpretation of Him, and then to build upon it even without being aware. And then worse, being human, one goes on to defend his wrong interpretation. And in addition to this, the current errors are undetected and deeply entrenched in the leadership of the church. This is reinforced by the eloquence and persuasive rhetoric of the best scholarly theologians. We owe much to academia and their endless pursuit of knowledge, but within the church of Jesus Christ there does exist essential elements brought to bear by the Holy Spirit, such as Bereanism, which differs strongly in motivation and procedure from institutes of higher learning.

In vain, we have attempted to bring up concerns to church leaders and academia of the inconsistencies of the current view of the Savior Jesus Christ, only to be mainly ignored. But when people listen at all, they tend to interrupt and miss the main points. The idea for the book came after years of thought and inquiry. Then I remembered what a very smart disciple of Christ said, "If you want to explain your position on an important issue do not argue it verbally, as you will only be exhausted and frustrated without ever making your point; write it out giving your whole view-point uninterrupted, this facilitates elucidation and avoids the unnecessary interruptions so that there is much less confusion."

The errors alluded to will be identified as we proceed. It is one thing to be wrong about an insignificant part of the Bible. But it should not be about the most glorious person who ever lived, the Lord Jesus Christ. God has allowed this to go on mostly unchecked ultimately I must believe for his own divine purpose. This anomaly is occurring in the church universally and seemingly undetected. Our study reveals that confusion has continued on through the centuries. The truth, correcting these errors if they are implemented, might just be to invigorate and prepare true believers for the great coming apostasy predicted in Scripture. We must arm ourselves with the correct vision and focus on the example the Holy Spirit gives us in our leader Jesus Christ. At present only portions of Christ's church suffer the persecution Jesus said would follow. This is due to the fact that not enough of us Christians are like Christ. If the man Jesus were timid like most of us they would not have murdered him

.

INTRODUCTION

The person of Christ has been written about often through the centuries. To begin with, we know that what the Old Testament prophets prophesied concerning Christ was accurate to the letter. Following the Old Testament prophesies we have the record of Christ's life in the gospels together with the epistles helping to interpret the life and implications of the work of Christ. But it doesn't end there because we are also given a good look at his ongoing life, especially in the book of revelation which Christ gave to the Apostle John. What is difficult to understand, is how there can be so much confusion. We do not want to place blame, but in a few cases we will need to identify the historical source of errors. Many have labored diligently to defend Biblical Christianity against speculative theology. We will affirm Evangelical Orthodoxy in its opposition to attacks on the Trinity and the deity of Christ, but we will also reveal and discuss more recent speculative developments concerning Christ's humanity which have found a comfortable home within today's church.

This work is primarily about the humanity of Jesus Christ, and we will extol equally the virtues of his humanity along with his deity. But we will give every effort to affirm the orthodoxy of the full deity and full humanity of Jesus in the one single person, Christ. The truth of Christ's deity should never be impugned while discussing his humanity, so when the context of any given passage focuses on his deity it shall be given the appropriate attention even though that is not the main focus of the book.

All that being said, we will look very closely at the true humanity of Christ Jesus that we feel is being misrepresented, and by extension his deity also being seen in the wrong light. This mysterious anomaly is being avoided by today's church. It is not being faced up to. His misunderstood and neglected humanity is this anomaly of which we speak, and it is the reason for, and the theme of this book.

It cannot be overstated that the humanity of Christ shares

equally in importance with his deity. They are equally rich in doctrinal truth and foundational to sound doctrine. In short the gospel of God will be able to go forth from the church unimpeded and with more divine blessing.

Beginning with a brief study of the Trinity of God (Chapter 1) we will see how Christ's humanity relates to the very nature of the one true God (Chapter 2). Then before advancing too far, we will find from Scripture itself the biblical doctrine of the humanity of Christ (Chapter 3). This inevitably will raise some reasonable questions in the reader's mind, since it is so foreign to current thinking, out of simple neglect, but the questions can be easily explained by the biblical doctrine of Christ's humanity (Chapter 4). Having laid the foundation for the biblical doctrine of Christ living as a man, we will discover there is a simple explanation for this profound truth which is found in the correct doctrine of Christ's humiliation and exaltation (Chapter 5). It tells us not only who He was and clarifies the incarnation but tells who He is today, and describes his ongoing heavenly work. Next we take a look at the office of Christ as prophet (Chapter 6). Christ's humanity has implications for the biblical doctrine of the Atonement which would be impossible unless He were a one hundred percent true man as well as one hundred percent God (Chapter 7). Finally all of the above will have applications to more fully understand Christ's sanctifying work, and assist the reader to understand the work of the Holy Spirit in conforming him to the image of God's Son (Chapter 8).

The intention here is to set forth accurately the biblical truth of the incarnation of the Son of God, including his humanity and his deity in their right perspectives. This will facilitate the Holy Spirit in manifesting the true glories of Jesus Christ to his followers. The glories of Christ's humanity have been a mystery far too long. Jesus is a delight to behold and even more delightful when He is known and beheld accurately.

1.

GOD – UNITY AND TRINITY

We hold that there is only one God who exists as one being. And we hold that within this one God there are three eternal and necessary distinctions, Father, Son, and Holy Spirit. But it is one thing to give lip service to this, and another thing to hold to it in reality. Because of the main subject of this book, and the tendency to misunderstand its purpose, it is necessary for us to demonstrate the unity and Trinity of God, and not just assume it, yet leave doubt in the reader's mind.

Now these things are not a matter of human speculation but established from Scripture itself.

Synopsis

(1) There is only one true God. All other so-called gods are nothings according to Scripture. The one true God is denominated "Jehovah" in the Old Testament, along with other divine names.

(2) The distinctions of Father, Son and Holy Spirit all relate in some way to the one true God.

(3) They not only relate to the one true God but specifically all have the divine attributes.

(4) God is not only the only God, but also one, not a corporation, partnership, or community of three individual Gods acting in unity. The plural Elohim is not a generic term for a tritheon.

(5) God is neither a tritheon of Gods nor a single person merely denominated as Father, Son, and Holy Spirit depending on different roles that the one God takes on. There are three distinctions in the one essence. And this cannot be described in creaturely terms. The three distinctions in one God is called Trinity, a triunity. And each

distinctly, essentially and eternally has all the divine attributes.

There has been considerable confusion in Christian writings concerning the Trinity of heaven, the Father, the Son, and the Spirit. Sometimes they are explained as three aspects of just one Person, using illustrations like the sun as having light, heat and power, or water existing in the states of solid ice, liquid water and gas as steam. This amounts to explaining that God is a Person who merely manifests Himself sometimes as Jesus, and sometimes as the Spirit, but then as the Father. This is wrong.

On the other hand, there have been continual attacks on the Trinity by those who consider Jesus but an exalted man and not God in the flesh. And the subtlety of this attack must be exposed without leaving the slightest doubt that Jesus is indeed the very incarnate one true God.

Much of this has already been collected in an admirable book on the Trinity by Edward Bickersteth back in 1892, and we cannot do much better in what follows than to use much of his wording to express the truth from Scripture accurately.

1. There is only one true God.

All other so-called gods are nothings according to Scripture. The one true God is denominated "Jehovah" in the Old Testament, along with other divine names.

Here we refer to the divine name "Jehovah", the term God applied and used interchangeably with the divine name, referring to the one true God, and how it is used in its plural form. We need to understand this.

In Scripture the most common designation that God gives for Himself is the Hebrew *JHWH*. given in the English Bibles by the word *LORD* in all capital letters, and sometimes Jehovah. This is his proper name. For example, In Deut 6:4 "Hear, O Israel: The LORD is our God, the LORD is one." Another way of translating it is "Hear O Israel, Jehovah is our God, Jehovah is one." Here we also see the word *God*. Sometimes as in chapter 1 He is referred

13

to by the word *God*. But right away in Gen 2:4 the word *LORD* (Jehovah), *JHWH,* appears right along with the word *God*. It shows that *LORD* (Jehovah, *JHWH*) is deity right from the beginning of the Bible. The reason the translators use the word *LORD* rather than Jehovah is that the exact pronunciation of the Hebrew of *JHWH* is not known, and in reading the Hebrew Bible Jews always said *Adonai* (the ordinary word for lord) when coming to *JHWH*. The Jews did not want people to pronounce the divine name, so they put the pronunciation marks for the vowels of *Adonai* with the letters of *JHWH*. Comparative Semitic studies would indicate a probable pronunciation of Yahweh or Yahveh.

This is the name God gives for Himself to distinguish Himself from false gods. False gods are often referred to in the plural form generically. But such gods (plural) cannot be confused with the one true God (plural) who in Scripture is also referred to with the word for a god but in the plural.

The Holy Spirit through his chosen Prophet Moses, when revealing the unmistakable truth of there being only one God, used the plural form *Elohim* for the one God. It is true that the most usual designation of the deity in the original Scriptures of the Old Testament is Elohim, which is mostly translated God, but it is the regular plural of Eloah, god. But Eloah for the one true God is much less frequent than in the plural form.

Not only that, this plural name is generally put in agreement with single verbs, pronouns, and adjectives, as in Genesis 1:1, "*Elohim* created." The word **created** in Hebrew is a verb indicating a plural subject doing the action of creating even though it is by the one true God and not a plurality of Gods. This is the ordinary construction through the whole Hebrew Bible. But sometimes the apposition is made not only with verbs, but pronouns, and adjectives in the plural likewise. For example with the pronoun **us** Gen 1:26 "And God (plural) said, Let us make man in our image."

On the other hand sometimes singulars and plurals are put together in the same statement. For example in Deut 5:26 "For who is there of all flesh, who has heard the voice (singular, not voices) of the living God (plural)." This also

14

occurs without the word Elohim. Psalm 149:2 "Israel shall rejoice in his maker (plural)." Also Isaiah 54:5 "for thy maker (plural) is thy husband (plural)." And Eccl. 12:1 "Remember thy creator "(plural).

What this means is that in God's self-revelation He displays something complex about Himself that requires the plural form of the word *God*.

This truth stands on the forefront of true faith: "I am God, and there is none else." Isaiah 46:9 "To the Alone, Supreme Jehovah."

This is the first and great commandment "Thou shall have none other gods but Me." And the response of every faithful worshiper is in the spirit of the Levitical adoration which is "O Lord our God, blessed be thy glorious name, which is exalted above all blessing and praise. Thou, even thou, art Lord alone: thou has made heaven, the heaven of heavens, with all their host, the earth, and all things that are therein, the seas, and all that is therein, and thou preserves them all; and the host of heaven worships thee. Thou art the Lord" Nehemiah 9:5 -7.

The one true Jehovah God compares Himself graphically to the idols and false gods who are nothings:

Psalm 115:3-8 "But our God is in heaven; He does whatever He pleases. 4, Their idols are silver and gold, the work of men's hands. 5, they have mouths, but they do not speak; eyes they have but they do not see; 6, they have ears, but they do not hear; noses they have but they do not smell; 7, they have hands, but they do not handle; feet they have, but they do not walk; nor do they mutter through their throat; 8, those who make them are like them; so is everyone who trusts in them."

Psalm 135:15-18 "The idols of the nations are silver and gold, the work of men's hands. They have mouths, but they do not speak; eyes they have but they do not see; 17, they have ears, but they do not hear; nor is there any breath in their mouths."

Deut 4:28 "And there you will serve god's, the work of men's hands, wood and stone, which neither see nor hear nor eat nor smell."

Psalm 31:6a "I have hated those who regard useless idols."

The nation of Israel was surrounded by nations who

believed in many gods or polytheism. They were in the midst of nations who were practicing idolatry, inventing new gods and by extension exporting them to other nations. But this is enough to establish how the one true Jehovah God views the gods of the nations.

2. There are in Scripture three distinctions relating to God.

The three distinctions of Father, Son and Holy Spirit all relate uniquely in some way to the one true God.

The word *father*, of course, is used of human fathers, but in some passages of the New Testament it clearly has reference to God. In the Old Testament God is referred to as the Father of the nation of Israel. But the name *Father* is used generally in the New Testament to refer to the one invisible God.

> Rom 1:7 "God our Father"; 1 Cor 1:3 "God our Father"; 2 Cor 1:2 "God our Father" 3, "Blessed be the God and Father of our Lord Jesus Christ, the Father of mercies and God of all comfort." Gal 1:1"God the Father." 3 "our God and Father." 1 Theses 1:1 "God the Father," and "God our Father." 1 John 1:3 "Our fellowship is with the Father and with His Son." Etc.

All of these passages identify the divine Father as God:

> 1 John 1:2 "eternal life which was with the Father and was manifested to us." 1 John 2:1 "And if anyone sins, we have an Advocate with the Father, Jesus Christ the righteous." 1 John 2:13 "I write to you, little children because you have known the Father." 1 John 2:15 "If anyone loves the world, the love of the Father is not in him." 1 John 2:16 "For all that is in the world-the lust of the flesh, the lust of the eyes, and the pride of life is not of the Father but is of the world."

The word *son*, of course, is used of human sons, but there are places where human beings, Christians, are called sons of God. This is without the slightest implication that Christians have been deified as gods.

> Rom 8:14 "For as many as are led by the Spirit of God, these are sons of God."

> Heb 12:7 "If you endure chastening, God deals with you as with sons; for what son is there whom a father does not chasten?"

16

Yet in many, many contexts the terms Son, Son of God, etc. are used of Christ and used directly in connection with God, with the Father, and with the Father and Holy Spirit.

> Matt 16:16 "Simon Peter answered and said, 'You are the Christ, the Son of the living God'." Mark 1:1 "The beginning of the gospel of Jesus Christ, the Son of God."

> 1 John 2:23 "Whoever denies the Son does not have the Father either; He who acknowledges the Son has the Father also."

In this last case "of God" is omitted.

Finally the word *spirit* can refer to invisible created beings, which from Scripture we understand to be either angels or demons, fallen angels. In addition there are references to the spirit of various men. But we find the term Spirit of God and Holy Spirit used to distinguish from other spirits. But there are times where because of the context the word *Spirit* is used alone and it must be understood to refer to the Holy Spirit. In addition, in the King James Version the archaic term Holy Ghost is used in place of Holy Spirit, but this is a mere translation matter.

> Heb 9:14 "How much more shall the blood of Christ, who through the eternal Spirit offered himself without spot to God."

> 1 Tim 3:16b God was manifest in the flesh, Justified in the Spirit, seen by angels"

What is clear is that in Scripture there are three designations that all relate to the one true God. And these three are joined together equally in many passages. Among the most outstanding are:

> Gen 1:1 "In the beginning God created the heavens and the earth. 2, The earth was without form, and void; and darkness was on the face of the deep. And the Spirit of God was hovering over the face of the waters." John 1:1-3 "In the beginning was the word, and the word was with God and the word was God. 2, He was in the beginning with God."

> Matt 3:16-17 "When He had been baptized, Jesus came up immediately from the water; and behold, the heavens were opened to Him, and He saw the Spirit of God descending like a dove and alighting on Him. 17, And suddenly a voice came from heaven, saying, 'This is my beloved Son in whom I am well pleased'."

> John14:16-17 "And I will pray the Father, and He will give you

another Helper, that He may abide with you forever-17, the Spirit of truth, whom the world cannot receive, because it neither sees Him nor knows Him; but you know Him, for He dwells with you and will be in you." Matt 28:19 "Go therefore and make disciples of all the nations, baptizing them in the name of the Father and the Son and of the Holy Spirit."

In addition there are passages indicating different ways in which the one God works:

1 Cor 12:4-6 "There are diversity of gifts, but the same Spirit. 5, There are differences of ministries, but the same Lord. 6, And there are diversities of activities, but it is the same God who works all in all."

1 Pet 1:2 "Elect according to the foreknowledge of God the Father, in sanctification of the Spirit, for obedience and sprinkling of the blood of Jesus Christ."

1 Pet 3:18 "For Christ also suffered once for sins, the just for the unjust, that He might bring us to God, being put to death in the flesh but made alive by the Spirit."

3. The three distinctions in God have divine attributes.

The distinctions of Father, Son, and Holy Spirit not only relate in some way to the one true God but specifically all have uniquely divine attributes.

It is not enough to affirm that the Father, Son, and Holy Spirit all relate uniquely to the one true God, because that would not necessarily mean that each were divine in nature. People have been so deceitful that they make professions that they believe that Jesus is the "Son of God" without accepting his true deity. When pressed they might equivocate by saying a very special man as a mere man could be claimed to be uniquely connected with the one true God without being divine. Or they could claim that a mere man could be given divine status without being God in his very nature. We specifically reject all these equivocations. And we will show it from Scripture.

What Scripture shows is that each of the three, Father, Son, and Holy Spirit specifically have uniquely divine attributes that are not found in created beings.

We must be careful about the meaning of the term *attribute*.

18

An attribute is something attributed to a person or thing. What is attributed may be something inherent to the person or thing but it is not limited to that. It may be something characteristic of persons because of what they do by a voluntary act of will, and therefore not an inherent property of their being. But they nevertheless give distinguishing characteristics about them.

And in considering the oneness and trinity of God we must not forget what Scripture declares about God's character and attributes in contrast to what it says about man. So first we identify those unique attributes. In the following we are simply transferring as cited by Edward Bickersteth from the King James Version, etc.

1. God's Omniscience.

All things naked to his eyes. Hebrews 4:13.

I the Lord search the heart. Jeremiah 17:10.

But the Lord looks on the heart. 1 Samuel 16:7.

2. God's Eternity

Thou art from everlasting. Psalm 43:2.

He inhabits eternity. Isaiah 57:15.

The eternal God Deuteronomy 33:27.

3. God's Omnipotence

With God all things are possible Matthew 19: 26.

The Lord God omnipotent. Revelation 19:6.

4. God's Omnipresence

The heaven of heavens cannot contain thee. 1 Kings 8:27.

5. God's Spirituality

God is a Spirit. John 4:24.

6. God's Eternal Sovereign Will

The counsel of Jehovah stands forever. The thoughts of his heart to all generations. Psalm 33:11.

The immutability of his counsel. Hebrews 4:17.

He turns wise men backward, and makes their knowledge foolish. Isaiah 64:25.

7. God's Infinite Glory

The glory of Jehovah shall endure forever. Psalm 104:31 .

8. God's Goodness

There is none good but one, that is, God. Matthew 19:17.

9. God's Purity And Holiness

God is light, and in him is no darkness at all. John 1:5.

10. God's Immortality

Who only hath immortality. 1 Timothy 6:16.

11. God's Self-Existence

The Father hath life in himself. John 5:26.

12. God The Creator

I have made the earth, and created man upon it. Isaiah 55:12.

He fashions the hearts (of the sons of men) alike. Psalm 33:15.

Woe unto him that strives with his Maker! Isaiah 45:9

So the one true God declares himself to be Self-Existent from eternity, Omnipresent, Immutable, Almighty, Incomprehensible, Omniscient, the Good One, the Holy One, the Creator, Preserver, and Administrator of all things in heaven and earth, the Searcher of hearts, and the most high Judge of all.

None of these apply to man but are all part of God's glory, which He declares He does not share with any other (Isaiah 42:8).

So now when we consider the three that are declared in Scripture to be uniquely associated with God, if they have the divine attributes that God does not share with any others, it demonstrates and proves that they are uniquely divine themselves.

We give here the biblical testimonies to the deity of all three within God: the Father, the Son, and the Holy Spirit, declaring that they equally are God.

Testimonies to the Deity of the Three Divine Persons

1. The Father, the Son, and the Holy Ghost are eternal.

(1) Father. I am the first, and I am the last. Isaiah 44:6. The everlasting God. Romans 16:26.

(2) Son. I am the first and the last. Revelation 1:17. Whose goings forth have been from of old, from everlasting. Micah 5:2.

(3) Spirit. The eternal Spirit. Hebrews 9:14.

The One Eternal is our trust. The eternal God is thy refuge, and underneath are the everlasting arms. Deuteronomy 33:27.

2. The Father, the Son, and the Holy Ghost created all things.

(1) Father. One God, the Father, of whom are all things. 1 Corinthians 8:6. The Lord.... it is he that hath made us. Psalm 100:3.

(2) Son. All things were made by him (the Word, etc. John 1:3). By him were all things created, etc. Colossians 1:16.

(3) Spirit. Who hath measured, etc. - who hath directed the Spirit of the Lord? Isaiah 40:13. The Spirit of God hath made me. Job 33:4.

The One Almighty is our trust. Commit the keeping of their souls to him, as unto a faithful Creator. 1 Peter 4:19.

3. The Father, the Son, and the Holy Ghost are omnipresent.

(1) Father. Do not I fill the heaven and earth? Said the Lord. Jeremiah 23:24.

(2) Son. Lo, I am with you always. Matthew 28:20.

(3) Spirit. Whither shall I go from thy Spirit? Psalm 139:7.

The One omnipresent God is our trust. He is not far from every one of us; for in him we live, and move, and have our being. Acts 17:27, 28.

4. The Father, the Son, and the Holy Ghost are incomprehensible and omniscient.

(1) Father. No one knows the Father, save the Son. Matthew 11:27. Known unto God are all his works, etc. Acts 15:18.

(2) Son. No one knows the Son, save the Father. Matthew 11:27. Lord, thou knows all things. John 21:17.

(3) Spirit. Who being his counselor hath taught him? Isaiah 40:13. The Spirit searches all things. 1 Corinthians 2:10.

We worship the One all-seeing God. All things are naked and opened unto the eyes of him with whom we have to do. Hebrews 4:13.

5. The Father, the Son, and the Holy Ghost are true, holy, and good.

(1) Father. He that sent me is true. John 7:28. Holy Father. Righteous Father John 17:11, 25. The Lord is good. Psalm 34:8.

(2) Son. I am ... . the truth. John 14:6. The Holy One and the just. Acts 3:14. The good Shepherd. John 10:11.

(3) Spirit. The Spirit is truth. 1 John 5:6. The Spirit, the holy One. John 14:26. Thy Spirit is good. Psalm 143:10.

We adore the One Lord of infinite goodness. Who shall not fear thee, Lord, and glorify thy name? For thou only art holy. Rev 15:4.

6. The Father, the Son, and the Holy Ghost have each a self-regulating will.

(1) Father. Him that works all things after the counsel of his own will. Ephesians 1:11.

(2) Son. The Son wills to reveal him. Matthew 11:27. Father, I will. John 17:24.

(3) Spirit. Dividing to every one severally as he wills. 1 Cor 12:11.

We rest on the will of him who alone is Jehovah. The will of the Lord be done. Acts 21:14.

7. The Father, the Son, and the Holy Ghost are the fountain of life.

(1) Father. With thee is the fountain of life. Psalm 46:9. God hath quickened us. Ephesians 2:4, 5.

(2) Son. In him (the Word) was life. John 1:4. The Son quickens whom he will. John 5:21 .

(3) Spirit. The Spirit is life. Romans 8:10. Born of the Spirit. John 3:8.

We depend on one life-giving God. Love the Lord thy God and cleave unto him, for he is thy life. Deuteronomy 30:20.

8. The Father, the Son, and the Holy Ghost strengthen, comfort, and sanctify us.

(1) Father. Thou strengthened me with strength in my soul. Psalm 138:3. I will comfort you. Isaiah 66:13.

Sanctified by God the Father. Jude 1:1.

(2) Son. I can do all things through Christ which strengthened me. Philippians 4:13. If any consolation in Christ.

Philippians 2:1. Sanctified in Christ Jesus. 1 Corinthians 1:2.

(3) Spirit. Strengthened with might by his Spirit in the inner man. Ephesians 3:16. The Comforter, the Holy Ghost.

John 14:26. Being sanctified by the Holy Ghost. Romans 15:16.

We trust in One God for spiritual power. My God, my strength, in whom I will trust. Psalm 18:2.

9. The Father, the Son, and the Holy Ghost fill the soul with Divine love.

(1) Father. Every one that loves him that begat. I John 5:1. If any man love the world, the love of the Father is not in him. 1 John 2:15.

(2) Son. The love of Christ constrains us. 2 Corinthians 5:14. If any man love not the Lord Jesus Christ. 1 Corinthians 16:22.

(3) Spirit. I beseech you for the love of the Spirit. Romans 15:30. Your love in the Spirit. Colossians 1:8.

The love of the One living and true God character lives the saint. Thou shall love the Lord thy God with all thy heart. Deut 6:5.

10. The Father, the Son, and the Holy Ghost gave the Divine law.

(1) Father. The law of the Lord is perfect. Psalm 19:7. The word of our God. Isaiah 40:8. Thus said the Lord God. Ezekiel 2:4.

(2) Son. The law of Christ. Galatians 6:2. The word of Christ. Colossians 3:16. These things said the Son of God. Revelation 2:18.

(3) Spirit. The law of the Spirit of life. Romans 8:2. Holy men of God spoke as they were moved by the Holy Ghost. 2 Peter 1:21. The Holy Ghost said. Acts 8:2.

The word of One Legislator is the believer's rule. There is one Lawgiver who is able to save. James 4:19.

11. The Father, the Son, and the Holy Ghost dwell in the hearts of believers.

(1) Father. I will dwell in them. 2 Corinthians 6:16. God is in you of a truth. 1 Corinthians 14:25. Our fellowship is with the Father. 1 John 1:3.

(2) Son. Christ may dwell in your hearts by faith. Ephesians 3:17. Christ in you, the hope of glory. Colossians 1:27. Our fellowship with Jesus Christ. 1 John 1:3.

(3) Spirit. The Spirit dwells with you, and shall be in you. John 14:17. The communion of the Holy Ghost. 2 Corinthians 13:14.

The contrite heart receives One Divine guest. Thus said the high and lofty One that inhabits eternity, I dwell with him that is of a contrite and humble heart. Isaiah 47:15 .

12. The Father, the Son, and Holy Ghost are each by himself, the supreme Jehovah and God.

(1) Father. I am Jehovah thy God. Exodus 20:2. Thou, Lord, art most High for evermore. Psalm 92:8.

(2) Son. Jehovah our God. Isaiah 40:3, with Matthew 3:3.

The Highest. Luke 1:76, with Matthew 11:10.

(3) Spirit. Jehovah God. Ezekiel 8:1,3. The Highest. Luke 1:35.

The One supreme Lord God is our God for ever and ever Jehovah, our Elohim, One Jehovah. Deuteronomy 6:4.

We see then that the Father, the Son, and the Holy Ghost, have the same divine attributes, concur with a mind and will and heart, personally independent but harmonious, in the same Divine acts, and are addressed by the same divine names.

In addition to the biblical proofs that the three designations, Father, Son and Holy Spirit all have the same divine attributes of the one God, we also have the additional affirmation of Jesus Himself to be God. Jesus attributed the divine name to Himself - before Abraham was I AM, etc. John 8:58. And Jesus accepted the worship of the Apostle Thomas of Him as "My Lord and my God." John 20:28

4. God is not a tritheon.

God is not one in the sense of a corporation, partnership, or community of three individual Gods acting in unity. We do not go into extended explanation, since the book is not intended to be a complete theological treatise. Deut 6:4 is sufficient to show that God is numerically one: "Hear O Israel: The Lord our God, the Lord is one." The plural Elohim is not a generic term for a tritheon, and indicates more than majesty. What is clear is that God within Himself is complex, as well as being a single being, as we already demonstrated.

5. The distinctions within God are essential, a true Trinity.

God is neither a tritheon of gods nor a single person merely denominated as Father, Son, and Holy Spirit depending on different roles that the one God takes on. There are three distinctions in the one essence. And this cannot be described in creaturely terms. The three distinctions in one God is called Trinity, a triunity. And each distinctly has all the

25

divine attributes. We understand the distinctness of Father, Son and Holy Spirit by the separate personal characteristics that they have, which is why the term *Persons* has been used of them, though in using that term there is no implication of them being separate beings.

Scripture shows separate personal characteristics. Foremost is the fact that the various Persons communicate with each other, indicating a separate "center of consciousness." If they are not distinct we would have the anomaly of a person talking to himself. Creatures might do that but not God.

The Son of God is not just another role that God the Father assumes in Christ's incarnation. This truth is easily proved with just a few of many Scriptures available.

At Christ's baptism.

> Matt 3:17 And behold, a voice out of the heavens, saying, This is MY beloved Son, in whom I am well pleased.

At Christ's transfiguration:

> Matt 17:5 While He was still speaking, behold a bright cloud overshadowed them; and behold a voice out of the cloud, saying, This is My beloved Son, with whom I am well-pleased; listen to Him.

Jesus says, in John 8:17-18 "Even in your law it has been written, that the testimony of two men is true. 18. I am He who bears witness of Myself, and the Father who sent Me bears witness of Me."

Jesus also said in John 6:38 "For I have come down from heaven, not to do My own will, but the will of Him who sent Me." The will, being the essence of personality certifies the distinction of the two, the Father and that of the Son. The above establishes from Scripture the Father and the Son are two of the distinctions emanating from the Trinity.

In conclusion, the Trinity of God and the unity of God picture our Triune God's glory. However, in the larger picture we must remember God said "I am the Lord, that is My name; I will not give My glory to another"(Isa 42:8). With that thought in mind we see God's glory shared equally by the Father, Son, and Holy Spirit, who together are the one true God. Likewise we are told in Deut 4:24 "For the

Lord your God is a consuming fire, a jealous God." This reinforces the idea He will not share His glory with another or if one were to exist, even another who is called God. This thought followed through to its conclusion means the three in fact are not three – not three gods - but one God who will not share his glory with anyone who is called God or who is called by any other name.

The Father is God, the Son Jesus is God, the Holy Spirit is God; they are the one and only Triune God who is one indivisible substance. Each distinction is Jehovah God, and there is no other Jehovah. Each is eternal; each is Governor; each is Creator; each is Sustainer - each shares all the glories of the one true God. We are to worship, obey and adore Father, Son and Holy Spirit equally. We are to worship, obey and adore no other god or creature.

We hold that there is only one God who exists as one being. And we hold that within this one God there are three eternal and necessary personal distinctions, Father, Son and Holy Spirit.

2.

CHRIST – GOD AND MAN

We have seen that Scripture teaches that the one God is a Trinity, with three personal distinctions within the divine being. These are God the Father, God the Son, and God the Holy Spirit. The man Jesus who lived on Earth as a Jew among Jews is without the slightest doubt identified with God the Son. This chapter deals with this truth, answering in what sense Jesus is identified with God the Son. Our answer is that Jesus is fully God and fully Man, the God-Man, the divine Son Himself come down incarnate as a true man as well as being God the Son.

But this is to be shown from Scripture. J. Greshem Machen pointed out long ago that there are self-professed Christians, we say Modernists, who say that Jesus was God, but denied He was born of a virgin, that He did miracles, that He died on the Cross as a penal substitute for the sins of men, and that He will come again in power and glory to earth. They denied fundamental teachings of the Christian faith. Modernists professed to be Christians, but were anything but. So saying that Jesus was God is no assurance that one holds to the truth of what Scripture means by Jesus being identified with God the Son.

Here we set forth what we hold to be the truth concerning Christ the God-Man and give our reasons from Scripture for rejecting the contrary. First we will state the truths in contrast to the error, then we will take up each of these to give the biblical reasons for rejecting the error. Finally, we will summarize with orthodox Christology and explain its importance to the subject of the book.

(1) Jesus is God the Son of the Trinity, fully God, not a man exalted in position to be equal with God so also called Son of Man.

(2) Jesus was God come down to earth and was not a man who became deified for the period of time of his life on earth and then lost his deity before dying.

(3) Jesus in his preexisting state before He became man was not a created being with divine attributes, but He was the uncreated God.

(4) Jesus came as a real man and was not a theophany.

(5) God the Son remained God in the incarnation and did not give up his deity or part of it to become the man Jesus and then take up his deity again afterward.

(6) In the incarnation, the divine Son of the Trinity took to Himself a true human nature without losing his divine nature, so his humanity was not a taking on real human flesh but without a true human nature, as some Kenoticists said.

(7) Jesus was fully God and fully Man, not partly God and partly man.

(8) Jesus was fully God and fully man in both his state of humiliation and his state of exaltation, not fully God in the state of exaltation but only partly God and fully man in his state of humiliation.

(9) The biblical facts require as a true statement that Christ Jesus was one undivided person, having a fully divine nature and a fully human nature without intermixture or confusion. He was not two persons, a divine person and a human person in one body.

Now we will proceed to restate these truths in brief, with the biblical proofs for them, but without extensive discussion that is found in theological texts on Christology. Often we will simply cite Bickersteth to whom we have referred previously and we have borrowed also from summary statements of another author.

1. Jesus is God the Son of the Trinity, not merely a man exalted in a position to be equal with God so also called Son of Man.

The Scriptures provide ample evidence that Christ is God. For example, the Scriptures testify to Christ possessing attributes that only God has: eternality (Isaiah 9:6; Micah 5:2; John 1:1; Colossians 1:17; Hebrews 1:8-10; Revelation 1:8), omnipresence (Matthew 18:20, 28:20; omniscience (John 21:17; Rev 2:23), omnipotence (Psalm 45:3;

Philippians 3:21; Revelation 1:8), immutability (Hebrews 13:8), self-existence (John 1:1-3, 5:21-26; Hebrews 7:16), and holiness (Luke 1:35; Acts 3:14; 1 Peter 1:19).

Eternality:

Isaiah 9:6 For unto us a child is born, unto us a son is given: and the government shall be upon his shoulder: and his name shall be called Wonderful, Counselor, The mighty God, The everlasting Father, The Prince of Peace.

Micah 5:2 But thou, Bethlehem Ephratah, *though* thou be little among the thousands of Judah, *yet* out of thee shall he come forth unto me *that is* to be ruler in Israel; whose goings forth *have been* from of old, from everlasting.

John 1:1 In the beginning was the Word, and the Word was with God, and the Word was God.

Colossians 1:17 And he is before all things, and by him all things consist.

Hebrews 1:8-10 But unto the Son *he saith*, Thy throne, O God, *is* for ever and ever: a sceptre of righteousness *is* the sceptre of thy kingdom. 9 Thou hast loved righteousness, and hated iniquity; therefore God, *even* thy God, hath anointed thee with the oil of gladness above thy fellows. 10 And, Thou, Lord, in the beginning hast laid the foundation of the earth; and the heavens are the works of thine hands:

Revelation 1:8 I am Alpha and Omega, the beginning and the ending, saith the Lord, which is, and which was, and which is to come, the Almighty.

Omnipresence:

Matthew 18:20 For where two or three are gathered together in my name, there am I in the midst of them.

Matthew 28:20 Teaching them to observe all things whatsoever I have commanded you: and, lo, I am with you always, *even* unto the end of the world. Amen.

Omniscience:

Revelation 2:23 And I will kill her children with death; and all the churches shall know that I am he which searcheth the reins and hearts: and I will give unto every one of you according to your works.

John 21:17 He saith unto him the third time, Simon, *son* of Jonas, lovest thou me? Peter was grieved because he said unto him the third time, Lovest thou me? And he said unto him, Lord, thou knowest all things; thou knowest that I love thee. Jesus saith unto him, Feed my sheep.

Omnipotence:

Psalms 45:3 Gird thy sword upon *thy* thigh, O *most* mighty, with thy glory and thy majesty.

Philippians 3:21 Who shall change our vile body, that it may be fashioned like unto his glorious body, according to the working whereby he is able even to subdue all things unto himself.

Immutability:

Hebrews 13:8 Jesus Christ the same yesterday, and to day, and for ever.

Self-Existence:

John 1:1-3 In the beginning was the Word, and the Word was with God, and the Word was God. 2 The same was in the beginning with God. 3 All things were made by him; and without him was not any thing made that was made.

John 5:21-26 For as the Father raiseth up the dead, and quickeneth *them*; even so the Son quickeneth whom he will. 22 For the Father judgeth no man, but hath committed all judgment unto the Son: 23 That all *men* should honour the Son, even as they honour the Father. He that honoureth not the Son honoureth not the Father which hath sent him. 24 Verily, verily, I say unto you, He that heareth my word, and believeth on him that sent me, hath everlasting life, and shall not come into condemnation; but is passed from death unto life. 25 Verily, verily, I say unto you, The hour is coming, and now is, when the dead shall hear the voice of the Son of God: and they that hear shall live. 26 For as the Father hath life in himself; so hath he given to the Son to have life in himself;

Hebrews 7:16 Who is made, not after the law of a carnal commandment, but after the power of an endless life.

Holiness:

Luke 1:35 And the angel answered and said unto her, The Holy Ghost shall come upon thee, and the power of the Highest shall overshadow thee: therefore also that holy thing which shall be born of thee shall be called the Son of God.

Acts 3:14 But ye denied the Holy One and the Just, and desired a murderer to be granted unto you;

1 Peter 1:19 But with the precious blood of Christ, as of a lamb without blemish and without spot:

Furthermore, the Lord Jesus Christ performed acts that only God can perform: creating (Hebrews 1:10; Colossians 1:15), and sustaining (Colossians 1:17; Hebrews 1:3).

Creating:

Hebrews 1:10 And, Thou, Lord, in the beginning hast laid the foundation of the earth; and the heavens are the works of thine hands:

Colossians 1:15 Who is the image of the invisible God, the firstborn of every creature:

Sustaining:

Colossians 1:17 And he is before all things, and by him all things consist.

Hebrews 1:3 Who being the brightness of *his* glory, and the express image of his person, and upholding all things by the word of his power, when he had by himself purged our sins, sat down on the right hand of the Majesty on high;

Also, Christ was given names and titles of deity: Son of God (Matthew 8:29, 16:16; Mark 1:1), and Lord and God (John 1:1,18; Hebrews 1:8; Titus 2:13; Matthew 22:43-45). Christ claimed to be God and He received worship (John 10:30; Matthew 4:10; John 5:23; Revelation 22:8-9; Philippians 2:10).

Matthew 8:29 And, behold, they cried out, saying, What have we to do with thee, Jesus, thou Son of God? Art thou come hither to torment us before the time?

Matthew 16:16 And Simon Peter answered and said, Thou art the Christ, the Son of the living God.

Mark 1:1 The beginning of the gospel of Jesus Christ, the Son of God;

John 1:1 In the beginning was the Word, and the Word was with God, and the Word was God.

John 1:18 No man hath seen God at any time; the only begotten Son, which is in the bosom of the Father, he hath declared *him*.

Hebrews 1:8 But unto the Son *he saith*, Thy throne, O God, *is* for ever and ever: a sceptre of righteousness *is* the sceptre of thy kingdom.

Titus 2:13 Looking for that blessed hope, and the glorious appearing of the great God and our Saviour Jesus Christ;

Matthew 22:43-45 He saith unto them, How then doth David in spirit call him Lord, saying, 44 The LORD said unto my Lord, Sit thou on my right hand, till I make thine enemies thy footstool? 45 If David then call him Lord, how is he his son?

John 10:30 I and *my* Father are one.

Matthew 4:10 Then saith Jesus unto him, Get thee hence, Satan: for it is written, Thou shalt worship the Lord thy God, and him only shalt thou serve.

John 5:23 That all *men* should honour the Son, even as they honour the Father. He that honoureth not the Son honoureth not the Father which hath sent him.

Revelation 22:8-9 And I John saw these things, and heard *them.* And when I had heard and seen, I fell down to worship before the feet of the angel which shewed me these things. 9 Then saith he unto me, See *thou do it* not: for I am thy fellow servant, and of thy brethren the prophets, and of them which keep the sayings of this book: worship God.

Philippians 2:10 That at the name of Jesus every knee should bow, of *things* in heaven, and *things* in earth, and *things* under the earth;

Let us accept the simple fact, as recorded in the Bible, of Christ's descent from above, that He, the Word, who in the beginning was with God and was God, was made flesh (John 1:1-14) and dwelt among us; that he came down from heaven; that he proceeded forth and came from God. And we must remember when He came from God, He forsook (John 8:42) the glory which he had with the Father before the world was; that being originally in the (John 17:5) form of God, He therefore preexisted before becoming man. And the reason given is that He came to save sinners that fallen men might be lifted up to God. He was more than man, and in fact God.

2. Jesus was God come down to earth and was not a man who became deified for the period of time of his life on earth and then lost his deity before dying.

This means that Christ existed before his earthly birth.

The scriptural evidence for this understanding of Christ

includes proof from the Old Testament (Isaiah 9:6), New Testament (John 8:58), Christ's involvement in the creation (Colossians 1:16) the appearance of the angel of the Lord (Exodus 3:2,4; Genesis 22:11), and by Christ's various names: Logos, Son of God, and Jehovah.

> Isaiah 9:6 For unto us a child is born, unto us a son is given: and the government shall be upon his shoulder: and his name shall be called Wonderful, Counselor, The mighty God, The everlasting Father, The Prince of Peace.

> John 8:58 Jesus said unto them, Verily, verily, I say unto you, Before Abraham was, I am.

> Colossians 1:16 For by him were all things created, that are in heaven, and that are in earth, visible and invisible, whether *they be* thrones, or dominions, or principalities, or powers: all things were created by him, and for him:

> Exodus 3:2 And the angel of the LORD appeared unto him in a flame of fire out of the midst of a bush: and he looked, and, behold, the bush burned with fire, and the bush *was* not consumed.

> Exodus 3:4 And when the LORD saw that he turned aside to see, God called unto him out of the midst of the bush, and said, Moses, Moses. And he said, Here *am* I.

> Genesis 22:11 And the angel of the LORD called unto him out of heaven, and said, Abraham, Abraham: and he said, Here *am* I.

Scripture is explicit that He was raised as a man who appeared to the disciples after his resurrection with a body.

> Lu 24:39 Behold my hands and my feet, that it is I myself: handle me, and see; for a spirit hath not **flesh and bones**, as ye see me have.

Moreover, the atoning death of Jesus as a mere man would not provide a sacrifice for the sins of any other than one other man, not the sins of many. Only the sacrifice of one who was both man and God would satisfy the justice of the infinite divine majesty.

3. Jesus in his preexisting state before He became man was not a created being with divine attributes, but He was the uncreated God.

We can almost immediately dismiss the heretical idea that Jesus in his preexisting state before He became man was a created being with divine attributes, because then there would be another god in addition to the one true Jehovah God and Jehovah declares that there is no other besides Him and none other shares his glory. This comes out in the fact that the Lord Jesus Christ who was declared to be the Son of God and Lord in Scripture is stated to be the exact same Jehovah God as in the Old Testament Scriptures. Hebrews 1:10 states: "And Thou, Lord, in the beginning hast laid the foundation of the earth; and the heavens are the works of thine hands." According to Hebrews this speaks of Christ, the Lord, but in the Old Testament passage from which this was taken (Psalm 102:25) the word *Lord* is the Hebrew *JHWH*. That means that the preincarnate Christ was not a demigod that created all else, but Jehovah God Himself.

4. Jesus came as a real man and not a theophany.

It might be supposed that He came without actually becoming a man. And this might be supposed to be given credence by the appearances of Jehovah God in the Old Testament. But Scripture declares God's Messiah would come as a man, with a human lineage and be born of a woman and so forth.

Christ's incarnation is defined as the eternal second Person of the Trinity taking on Himself humanity or flesh. The central supporting passage for the incarnation is John 1:14: "The Word became flesh and made his dwelling among us. We have seen his glory, the glory of the One and Only, who came from the Father, full of grace and truth." The means of Christ's incarnation is the virgin birth (Matthew 1:23, Luke 1:35).

> John 1:14 And the Word was made flesh, and dwelt among us, (and we beheld his glory, the glory as of the only begotten of the Father,) full of grace and truth.

> Matthew 1:23 Behold, a virgin shall be with child, and shall bring forth a son, and they shall call his name Emmanuel, which being interpreted is, God with us.

> Luke 1:35 And the angel answered and said unto her, The Holy Ghost shall come upon thee, and the power of the Highest shall overshadow thee: therefore also that holy thing which shall be born of thee shall be called the Son of God.

We give what Bickersteth says:

"The Word was made flesh, and dwelt among us." (John 1:14). There is a majestic condescension in these few words that nothing can equal. He was made man. [Then] He died, but rose again, that he might be the Lord of both the dead and the living; and he ascended to his Father and our Father, to his God and our God. This was the man Christ Jesus: a man (Acts 2:22) demonstrated from God by miracles, and prodigies, and signs, which God did by him: a man ordained by (Acts 17:31) God, to be the judge of the living and the dead.

Believe me; we yield to none in the strength of conviction with which we hold to the humanity of Jesus Christ. "The Word was made flesh, and dwelt among us." We take our stand fearlessly on this. How otherwise could such a relationship have been expressed than in such or such like words - "There is one God and one mediator betwixt God and men, the man Christ Jesus; who gave himself (1 Timothy 2:5,6) a ransom for all?" Having descended with the express design of doing his Father's pleasure, of serving a perfect service, of rendering a spotless obedience to the law, of exhibiting a Divine model of self denial. How otherwise could he declare his mission than in these or similar terms. "I came down from heaven, not to do mine own will, but the will of him (John 6:38) that sent me?" Standing forth the Author and Finisher of the faith. The exemplar of that (Hebrews 1 1 :2) faith we are to Copy; AS MAN, working his miracles not by virtue of his Divinity ever inherent in him, but by virtue of a perfect faith in the power of the Father. That faith which with us is intermittent and often overborne, being with him constant without defect, and victorious without defeat; how otherwise could he reveal the secret and entire dependence of his soul on God, than in language such as this, "I can of mine own self do nothing. (John 5:30)." "The Father that dwells (John 5:30) in me, he does the works?" (John 14:10).

We agree with Bickersteth. This contrasts with theophanies in which God came temporarily down to earth, and it contrasts with the pagan gods that came among men. This is an incarnation of God in human flesh, as Scripture declares.

The Word, which was with God and was God, became flesh and dwelt among us (John 1:1, 14). He dwelt permanently, was born, lived, and died.

5. Jesus was truly God before the incarnation but did not give up his deity or part of it to become the man Jesus and then take up his deity again afterward.

Being God the Son He does not change in his being in any way. We already pointed out his immutability.

6. In the incarnation, the divine Son of the Trinity took to Himself a true human nature without losing his divine nature, so his humanity was not a taking on real human flesh but without a true human nature.

That Christ was human is clear from the Scriptures. He was born and had a human body, as described in the Gospels (see also Galatians 4:4), He had a human soul and spirit, He exhibited the characteristics of a human being, like growing up (Luke 2:52).

> Galatians 4:4 But when the fulness of the time was come, God sent forth his Son, made of a woman, made under the law,

> Luke 2:52 And Jesus increased in wisdom and stature, and in favor with God and man.

Only by being fully human could Christ provide an example for our lives, provide an effective sacrifice for sin, be able to fulfill the Davidic covenant and be able to be a sympathetic high priest.

We repeat Bickersteth again:

> In the Old Testament, as man [He is] the seed of the woman [that is] bruised in his heel: as God he achieves a victory surpassing human strength, he bruises the (Genesis 3:15) serpent's head. Against him as man, we read in the second Psalm, the kings of the earth set themselves: to him as the anointed Son of God, Divine royalty is (Psalm 2:2, 7, 12) ascribed and universal trust attracted. As man he appears at the close of the second Psalm, like a weary traveler, drinking of the wayside brook and revived therewith; but the opening verses describe him as the victorious Lord of all on the throne with Jehovah.

If you regard his humanity, He is "Unto us a child is born" (Isaiah 9:6); if you regard his Deity, his name is the Mighty God. As David's son, he is the rod out of the stem of Jesse: as David's Lord, he shall smite the earth with the rod of his mouth, and with the breath of his lips shall he slay the wicked. In respect of his manhood, he grows up as a tender plant, despised and rejected. In virtue of his Godhead, he bears the iniquity of us all, and (Isaiah 53:3, 6) with his stripes we are healed. As man, he is the pierced, smitten shepherd: as God, he is Jehovah's (Zechariah 7:10) fellow (Zechariah 8:7).

Just as we read, Jesus increased in wisdom, and (Luke 2:52) therefore there were subjects unknown to him at twelve years of age, which were acquired by him or revealed to him afterwards: so in Mark 13:32 Jesus is speaking in his human nature. This point was not made known to him as man, but by the Spirit. And since his manhood is spoken of as a condition of his prophetical office (Deuteronomy 18:15, of thy brethren) he is declaring as an ambassador what lay within his commission, and this day and hour he was not empowered as a prophet to reveal.

So says Bickersteth.

In all of this Jesus must have had a true human nature. He could not have been merely God taking on human flesh alone, without actually becoming man. Moreover one who was not a man could never be a sacrificial substitute for **men** to pay the penalty for the sins of **men**.

7. Jesus was fully God and fully Man, not partly God and partly man.

The declaration of Scripture that Jesus came forth from God is significant in understanding the issue here. In understanding Christ's Person, when we remember Christ's descent from above, we realize that it was He, the Word, who in the beginning was with God and was God, who was made flesh (John 1:1-14) and dwelt among us, that he came down from heaven, that he proceeded forth and came from God. So personhood of the incarnate Son of God derives from God, rather than man. The same Person who existed from eternity prior to the incarnation continued in human flesh in the incarnation. No new person was created from his human nature. The divine nature continued unchanged and a human nature was added, so that the same Person that existed before had new human attributes, without any change in his divine attributes. The confusion comes about by thinking that two natures imply two personal aspects to Christ that can be thought of separately. This is incorrect.

But if part God and part man, Christ could not be a substitutionary sacrifice for man on the one hand nor on the other hand would his sacrifice satisfy the justice of God.

8. Jesus was fully God and fully man in both his state of humiliation and his state of exaltation. He was not fully God only in the state of exaltation but partly God and fully man in his state of humiliation.

As we will show more fully in examining Scripture on the exaltation of Christ (Chapter 5), the incarnation itself does not imply any loss of divine attributes. But the idea here of being partly God and then later fully God impugns the immutability of Christ. This heretical idea was introduced by the Kenoticists and is a very serious error. When we say that Jesus in his state of humiliation refrained from the exercise of his divine attributes that in no way implies that He did not have them. Not using them was entirely voluntary on his part.

9. The biblical facts require as a true statement that Christ Jesus was one undivided person having a fully divine nature and a fully human nature without intermixture or confusion. He was not two persons, a divine person and a human person in one body.

In addition to the Biblical evidence for Christ's deity and humanity, the unity of these natures in the person of Christ is also evident (John 1:14; Galatians 4:4; 1 Timothy 3:16; Ephesians 2:16-18; 1 John 2:1-2, 4:2, 4:15, 5:5).

> John 1:14 And the Word was made flesh, and dwelt among us, (and we beheld his glory, the glory as of the only begotten of the

Father,) full of grace and truth.

Galatians 4:4 But when the fulness of the time was come, God sent forth his Son, made of a woman, made under the law,

1 Timothy 3:16 And without controversy great is the mystery of godliness: God was manifest in the flesh, justified in the Spirit, seen of angels, preached unto the Gentiles, believed on in the world, received up into glory.

Ephesians 2:16-18 And that he might reconcile both unto God in one body by the cross, having slain the enmity thereby: 17 And came and preached peace to you which were afar off, and to them that were nigh. 18 For through him we both have access by one Spirit unto the Father.

1 John 2:1-2 My little children, these things write I unto you, that ye sin not. And if any man sin, we have an advocate with the Father, Jesus Christ the righteous: 2 And he is the propitiation for our sins: and not for ours only, but also for *the sins of* the whole world.

1 John 4:2 Hereby know ye the Spirit of God: Every spirit that confesseth that Jesus Christ is come in the flesh is of God:

1 John 4:15 Whosoever shall confess that Jesus is the Son of God, God dwelleth in him, and he in God.

1 John 5:5 Who is he that overcometh the world, but he that believeth that Jesus is the Son of God?

Scripture does not speak of Christ acting in one nature or the other. Both natures apply to the God-Man, as expressed in Acts 20:28 and 1 Cor 2:8. "God purchased the church with his own blood." The world crucified the Lord of glory, God Himself in Christ. How can God have blood and be crucified? Only if it is Christ's person that is the focus, and not two natures separated out.

All of the above is essentially stated in the historical definition made at the council of Chalcedon, in the early history of the church.

The Chalcedonian Definition or Creed

The Chalcedonian Creed is a statement by the early church stating the truth about the Person of the Lord Jesus Christ in contrast to errors up to the time it was formulated. It can be seen that it incorporates in different language the 9 points that we have given in this chapter.

"We, then, following the holy fathers, all with one consent, teach men to confess, one and the same Son, our Lord Jesus Christ; the same perfect in Godhead and also perfect in Manhood; truly God, and truly Man, of a reasonable soul and body; consubstantial with the Father according to the Godhead, and consubstantial with us according to the Manhood; in all things like unto us without sin; begotten before all ages of the Father according to the Godhead, and in these latter days, for us and our salvation, born of Mary the virgin Mother of God according to the Manhood. He is one and the same Christ, Son, Lord, Only-begotten, existing in two natures without mixture, without change, without division, without separation, the diversity of the two natures not being at all destroyed by their union, but the peculiar properties of each being preserved, and concurring to one person and one subsistence, not parted or divided into two persons, but one and the same Son, and Only-begotten, God the Word, and as the Lord Jesus Christ Himself hath taught us, and as the Creed of the holy fathers has delivered to us."

We provide the following interpretation of the creed, to summarize the points of this chapter.

We, then, following the holy fathers, all with one consent, teach men to confess, one and the same Son, our Lord Jesus Christ;

Meaning: God the Son when He became a man, taking into himself the form of man, remained the same Son and in no way did He become a different person, leaving or changing/altering who He was resulting in two Sons, but remained permanently the same eternal Person when permanently taking into Himself human flesh.

The same perfect in Godhead and also perfect in manhood;

truly God, and truly Man,

Meaning: when God the Son condescended to become man, Jesus the Christ, He remained perfect God and became perfect man as well. He did not change his status as God nor did He become any kind of a hybrid, but truly a man with only the normal human abilities.

Of a reasonable soul and body;

Meaning: the same reasonable soul and body configuration as any other human being; the ability to reason and will, and to use human senses and perceive and judge facts.

Consubstantial with the Father according to the Godhead, and consubstantial with us according to the Manhood;

Meaning: of the same substance or nature as God and the same substance or nature as us humans.

In all things like unto us without sin;

Meaning: the absence of sin in eternity and no imputed original sin nor guilt from original sin, nor guilty of committing any sins of any kind during his life. And not until the sins of the many who believed and who would believe in Him were imputed to Him on the Cross would He be found guilty of those sins and justly punished by God the Father.

Begotten before all ages of the Father according to the Godhead, and in these later days for us and our salvation, born of Mary the virgin Mother of God according to the Manhood.

Meaning: He was eternally begotten and is eternally of the substance of God and who therefore is God, and in time was born of a human virgin and is of her human or same substance as well.

He is one and the same Christ, Son, Lord, Only-begotten,

Meaning: although Christ was born in time and his person is the same person who is anchored in eternity, He was the Son in eternity and is continuing as the same Son, and there is no other begotten Son.

Existing in two natures

Meaning: He, the one person Christ, lives and exists having two natures, one divine and the other human. One of the natures is from one of the distinctions of the Trinity and the other is from the dust/substance of Mary, born out of the miraculous conception.

Without mixture,

Meaning: the two natures and their respective abilities do not mix or blend nor are they communicated from one nature to the other nature.

Without change,

Meaning: the divine nature did not change into the human nature nor did the real human nature of Christ change or become in any way deified. Neither did either nature change into a blending of natures, an alien being of some kind, for example, half God and half man, or one third God, man and angel. The two natures did not alter.

Without division,

Meaning: Christ the Son of God never acted as two separate persons nor was He ever divided within Himself. Whatever He did was ascribed to the one person; the two natures did not result in a division of his person.

Without separation,

Meaning: the two natures were never separated so as to conclude something was done by one of the natures rather than by the person. We cannot say or conclude something was done by one of Christ's natures because a nature is not a person. The two natures of Christ are joined inseparably together in one person.

The diversity of the two natures not being at all destroyed by their union, but the peculiar properties of each being preserved, and concurring to one person and one substance, not parted or divided in to two persons, but one and the same Son, and Only-begotten, God the Word, and as the Lord Jesus Christ Himself hath taught us, and as the Creed of the holy fathers has delivered to us.

Meaning: in summary of what has already been concluded and said above affirming the existence of the two natures in

43

the one person being indissolubly joined together in perfect union, that it does not destroy the diversity and distinction of the two natures or the one person, Christ our Lord.

Kenoticism

We must pay particular attention to the heresy of Kenoticism. Any suggestion that in the incarnation Christ was anything less than true God, the very Son of God, must be rejected in the most determined way. The errors of the Kenoticists arose directly out of a concern to uphold the true humanity of Christ but then fell into serious error. It began with German rationalism which infected theological thinking at the time. They could not conceive how to harmonize the attributes of God with human attributes. It started with the concept that the Son of God could still be God with only some of the divine attributes that were thought to be incompatible with human attributes. Appendix B deals with the heresy of Kenoticism.

In our treatment of the humanity of Christ we make it very clear that we hold that absolutely none of the inherent divine attributes or properties of deity are in any way diminished by the incarnation. We hold the full and complete position given in the Chalcedonian formula.

3.

THE BIBLICAL DOCTRINE

The subject of the book is the humanity of Christ. This chapter deals with the biblical truth of Jesus Christ living his life as a man, a man made like his brethren, just as the writer of Hebrews tells us. He is a man just as much as He is God. This is made clear to us in the previous chapter. Also He will continue to exist forever as God while remaining a true man.

Scripture declares Christ to be a man in 1 Tim 2:5 "For there is one God, and one mediator between God and men, the man Christ Jesus." Pilate also called Jesus a man in John 19:5 "behold the man," as did Peter in Acts 2:22 "Jesus the Nazarene, a man", and there are many such passages which affirm this same thing. Scripture would be wrong if it continually called Jesus a man if he was not truly a man; it declares him not less than a man or more than a man. Scripture never portrays him as some kind of angelic being or super-human man. He is in fact both God and man, not part God and part man, but fully God and fully man.

We call Him the God-Man. This truth, while it might in part remain a mystery, is according to Heb 2:17, a necessary portion of the body of Christian doctrines, or to say it another way, it was prerequisite to his ministry of redemption. In order for Christ Jesus to become the mediator between God and man and to make propitiation for the sins of the people, it was biblically necessary for the Savior of the world to be both God and man. It was not just the best of three or four possible options that God had at his disposal, but it was the only possible option for God to be consistent with who He is and not violate his character. So therefore in the fulness of time, according to his love and mercy, it was his best solution!

We will see that without question Scripture teaches the following truths concerning Jesus during the state of his humiliation:

1. Jesus grew in wisdom and knowledge as a boy into manhood.

2. Jesus was born of a woman under the Law living in complete obedience to it.

3. Jesus lived as a man in dependence on God, Father and Holy Spirit, living in the fulness of the Holy Spirit.

4. The miracles Jesus did were the miracles of God the Father worked by the power of the Holy Spirit.

5. The perfect and sinless Jesus was brought to perfection through living out his life as a man.

6. Jesus lived his life on earth by faith and not by sight.

7. What Jesus taught He received from God the Father and not from Himself.

1. Jesus grew in wisdom and knowledge as a boy into manhood.

Scripture teaches Jesus was a normal boy differing in the way he lived from other boys only because He was filled with the Spirit and without any sin. Jesus' life as an infant and a toddler and a young man are explained in Luke 2:40 "And the Child continued to grow and become strong, increasing in wisdom; and the grace of God was upon Him." The use of the word *continued* implies Jesus as a toddler was already growing and becoming strong. We see then, from his birth to age twelve, indicated in v 42, that He was continuing to grow. We are not told to what level or degree He reached in his growth, but we do know that He was far ahead of his peers because the teachers were amazed. From v 47 we read "And all who heard Him were amazed at his understanding and his answers." And this was when He was twelve. They would not have been amazed if He were not very advanced in his study. The only other supposition is that what He knew was by the exercise of his divine attributes. But this is directly contrary to the statement that He **grew** in wisdom, which makes that supposition impossible. Yes, He was accomplished to such a degree not because He was God but because He had become disciplined and had learned to apply Himself in his studies as a boy. Of course He did have one advantage, not having the normal distractions which belong to a fallen mind. He had no sin nature, so there was not that distraction to impede his growth as would occur with a sinful child. This was true of Him as a toddler as well as a young boy of twelve. Yet, He would still have to increase in knowledge and wisdom without the use of divine abilities. Did Jesus have perfect recall in his early stages of development as some humans are known to have? We are not told. It is reasonable to assume that a perfect human mind would have perfect recall. Nevertheless Jesus was increasing and becoming strong. In other words, there was a process of development taking place in his early life. The natural implication of this passage in Luke is that He was born with the need to learn and grow through his every day experiences. Another way of putting it a little more directly is that Jesus did not access his omniscience or omnipotence, which if employed, Scripture could not say He was growing or learning.

Also it is important to note that Jesus had not reached complete accomplishment by the age of twelve because of what the Holy Spirit tells us in v 51 and v 52: "And He went down with them, and came to Nazareth; and He continued in subjection to them; and his mother treasured all these things in her heart. And Jesus kept increasing in wisdom and stature, and in favor with God and men." Jesus kept increasing in wisdom and stature and in favor with God and men, and Scripture is absent of any comment as to how long He continued to increase that way. Yet it would be very important to know and to understand just how long He grew in favor with God and men to complete our picture of his person. He not only grew in wisdom but also in favor, meaning that in some sense he was maturing spiritually as a man. Growing in favor as God the Son just does not make sense and is impossible.

2. Jesus was born of woman under the Law living in complete obedience to it.

Scripture says concerning the coming of Christ as a man:

> Gal 4:4 But when the fulness of the time was come, God sent forth his Son, made of a woman, made under the law, 5 To redeem them that were under the law, that we might receive the adoption of sons.

We understand that God sent God the Son into the world, born of the Virgin Mary as the incarnate God-Man. But Gal 4:4-5 says something more, that the God-Man was born **under the Law**. That means that Jesus fulfilled his life on earth as a man under the law, keeping it perfectly. James 2:10 tells us that not keeping it at just one point makes one guilty "of all":

> James 2:10 For whosoever shall keep the whole law, and yet offend in one point, he is guilty of all.

But there is more to keeping law than merely not breaking it at any point. A perfect righteous life is needed. That means living as a man under the law at all times.

In what sense was Jesus under the law? Did it include the Mosaic Law? Jesus said:

> Matt 5:17 Think not that I am come to destroy the law, or the prophets: I am not come to destroy, but to fulfill. 18 For verily I say unto you, Till heaven and earth pass, one jot or one tittle shall in no wise pass from the law, till all be fulfilled.

> Luke 16:17 And it is easier for heaven and earth to pass, than one tittle of the law to fail.

Jesus was referring to the Mosaic Law here by referring to jots and tittles. He was a Jew under the Mosaic Law as well as the universal moral law of God.

To not keep the law or violate it is sin, and Jesus was sinless. So Jesus kept the law, and He kept the law as a Jew born under the Law of Moses, of which Jesus Himself said that not the least little bit could fail. In this, Jesus was a man obligated to every little detail of law as it truly was in the Word of God.

Jesus then fully fulfilled the obligation laid down in the Word of God to be a man under the law in every sense.

3. Jesus lived as a man in dependence on God, Father and Holy Spirit, living in the fulness of the Holy Spirit.

First Jesus Himself said that He came to do the will of God, the one who sent Him:

> John 5:30 I can of mine own self do nothing: as I hear, I judge: and my judgment is just; because I seek not mine own will, but the will of the Father which hath sent me.

But we read also of references to the Holy Spirit in connection with Jesus:

> Isaiah 42:1 "Behold, My Servant, whom I uphold; My chosen One in whom My soul delights, I have put my Spirit upon Him; He will bring forth justice to the nations".

> Isaiah 59:20-21: "And a Redeemer will come to Zion, And to those who turn from transgression in Jacob, declares the Lord. 21 And as for Me, this is My covenant with them, says the Lord: My Spirit which is upon you, and My words which I have put in your mouth, shall not depart from your mouth, nor from the mouth of your off spring, nor from the mouth of your off spring's offspring, says the Lord, from now and forever."

First in Isaiah it is said of the Messiah/Christ that God's Spirit is **upon** Him.

We must ask what it means for the Spirit of God to be upon a person. It was spoken of those who were empowered and controlled by the Spirit of God to do or say something that God wanted to be said or done. And this was spoken of human instruments of God.

> Isaiah 11:2-3 "And the Spirit of the Lord will rest on Him, the spirit of wisdom and understanding, the spirit of council and strength, The spirit of knowledge and the fear of the Lord".

We notice that what was true of other human instruments of God was to be true of Jesus, the promised Messiah.

But the prophecy concerning Christ the Messiah states not only that the Spirit of God will rest on Him but that He will live in the fear of the Lord. This is not something spoken of God but something of Jesus as man. So the Spirit of God on Jesus meant, as it always had, that a man would live according to the will of God.

And this is what we see throughout Jesus' life:

> Matt 3:16 -17 "And after being baptized, Jesus went up immediately from the water; and behold, the heavens were opened, and he saw the Spirit of God descending as a dove, and coming upon Him, 17. and behold, a voice out of the heavens, saying, This is My beloved Son, in whom I am well pleased."

> (Also Mark 1:9-10, and Luke 3:1-22)

> Mark 1:12: "And immediately the Spirit impelled Him to go out into the wilderness."

Luke 4:1: " And Jesus full of the Holy Spirit, returned from the Jordan and was led about by the Spirit in the wilderness."

Luke 4:14: "And Jesus returned to Galilee in the power of the Spirit."

We note in Scripture additional passages affirming the Holy Spirit working in the life of Christ during his state of humiliation while on earth.

Heb 9:14 "How much more will the blood of Christ, who through the eternal Spirit offered Himself without blemish to God."

The eternal Spirit here is distinguished from the spirit of Christ Himself. Only the Holy Spirit is both eternal and distinct from Him. So it ought to be taken to be the Holy Spirit. Jesus having been endowed with the Holy Spirit without measure (John 3:34) in preparation for his life's work, certainly received all of the graces necessary to carry Him all through his ministry and ultimately to its completion, as in the case with ordinary men. The phrase "without blemish" includes the divine influence of the Holy Spirit not only at the critical hour of crucifixion, but throughout the process by which Christ Jesus always lived his life and acted perfectly (without fault), fulfilling all of the law of God, and finally voluntarily offering Himself as a spotless sacrifice to God. His sacrifice was accomplished not in his own strength but through his submitting to his Father by the eternal Holy Spirit, achieving perfect propitiation to God for the people. Even Christ's sacrifice was accomplished through the Holy Spirit. And this is where one would otherwise expect Jesus to act entirely on his own.

Isaiah 11:1-4 is one of many passages which prophesies and corroborates the above:

Isaiah 11:1 And there shall come forth a rod out of the stem of Jesse, and a Branch shall grow out of his roots: 2 And the spirit of the LORD shall rest upon him, the spirit of wisdom and understanding, the spirit of counsel and might, the spirit of knowledge and of the fear of the LORD; 3 And shall make him of quick understanding in the fear of the LORD: and he shall not judge after the sight of his eyes, neither reprove after the hearing of his ears: 4 But with righteousness shall he judge the poor, and reprove with equity for the meek of the earth:

50

He not only is quick in understanding in the fear of the LORD as a man, but He does not judge by his own sight and hearing, but by the guidance of the Spirit of God, as the text says.

What happened in Jesus' life at the beginning of his ministry confirms that He continued in dependence on God:

> Matt 4:1 Then Jesus was led up by the Spirit into the wilderness to be tempted by the devil.

Immediately, following his baptism we see Jesus depending on the Holy Spirit leading Him. And this continued throughout the four gospels. The Holy Spirit did not just start Jesus on the right track.

4. The miracles Jesus did were the miracles of God the Father worked by the power of the Holy Spirit.

What does Scripture say concerning the way in which Jesus did miracles? Not only Scripture elsewhere, but also Jesus Himself says how they took place.

The teaching of Scripture elsewhere

First consider what Scripture says elsewhere:

> Acts 2:22 "Men of Israel, listen to these words: Jesus the Nazarene, a man attested to you by God with miracles and wonders and signs which God performed through Him in your midst, just as you yourselves know."

Peter in beginning his apostolic ministry starting with his first sermon makes doubly sure that Jesus is first known as a man, a local man from Nazareth, not some kind of angel or alien being, and second, that the miracles, wonders, and signs which this man Jesus did were in fact performed by God as distinct from Jesus Himself. The point Peter is making here is all encompassing and establishes an important truth for the foundation of the gospel which follows in his sermon.

When Peter said God performed through Jesus he was not saying anything more than could be said of God working through Moses and Elijah who themselves did not perform their miracles in their own strength, but God did the miracles through them.

What Peter says is of the utmost importance because He is making a general statement concerning the entire ministry of Jesus during his life on earth. He says that **God**, in clear distinction from Jesus, **did the performing.**

> Acts 10:38 " You know of Jesus of Nazareth, how God anointed Him with the Holy Spirit and with power, and how He went about doing good, and healing all who were oppressed by the devil; for God was with Him".

We see the same thing stated or implied many times:

> John 10:32 I showed you many good works from the Father; for which of them are you stoning Me?

The good works performed as miracles were **from** the Father, not Himself.

> John 14:11-12 Believe Me that I am in the Father, and the Father in Me; otherwise believe on account of the works themselves. 12. Truly, truly, I say to you, he who believes in Me, the works that I do shall he do also; and greater works than these shall he do; because I go to the Father.

Jesus is telling the disciples they will work their miracles just as He did, in God's power and not in their own strength. He is making a direct comparison between what they will do and what He Himself did. Many miracles were done by the disciples fulfilling Jesus' words to the letter.

> Luke 5:17 And it came about one day that He was teaching; and there were some Pharisees and teachers of the law sitting there, who had come from every village of Galilee and Judea and from Jerusalem; and the power of the Lord was present for Him to perform healing.

Luke makes sure it is understood it was in the power of God that Jesus performed the miracle of healing and not his own power. Jesus by virtue of being God in the flesh inherently had the ability to heal but instead Scripture very clearly states the power of the Lord was present as distinct from Jesus Himself. We notice that Jesus always acted in every situation not in his own power but always in the power of the Holy Spirit.

> Acts 10:38 "You know of Jesus of Nazareth, how God anointed Him with the Holy Spirit and with power, and how He went about doing good, and healing all who were oppressed by the devil; for God was with Him."

This statement by Peter is more general in his statement that Jesus went about doing good, such could include healing Peter's mother-in-law of her fever, turning water into wine, raising the dead, casting out demons, and so forth. It encompasses all kinds of supernatural power.

The very fact that God anointed Jesus with the Spirit to perform these supernatural acts doesn't make sense if Jesus did them through accessing his own inherent powers. But Peter makes clear that we are to know and understand that it was God – the Father and the Holy Spirit – that was with Jesus of Nazareth giving Him the power, as Peter said.

Jesus' Own Teaching

What did Jesus say about how He performed his miracles? When accused of casting out demons by the prince of demons, Jesus did not say that it was by his own power, but that the accusation was an attack on the Holy Spirit. This is reported in Matt 12:14-37, Mark 3:22-30, and Luke 11:14-23. This is familiar as the blaspheming of the Holy Spirit and the unpardonable sin. In all three passages Jesus had just cast out a demon from a man who was blind and dumb and was then accused by the Pharisee's of working in the power of Satan. And Jesus replied to them (Luke 11:20): "But if I cast out demons by the finger of God, then the kingdom of God has come upon you." He says directly that it was by the finger of God. But being God Himself, it might be supposed that in saying this He was referring to his own power. But we see from what follows that this is incorrect. He went on to say their accusation was a direct blasphemy not of Himself but the Holy Spirit. He was giving credit to the Holy Spirit for casting out the demon. They accused Him of working in the power of Satan when in fact He was working in the power of the Holy Spirit, and that is what made it a blasphemy that would not be forgiven them. There is no mistaking the source of power for the miracles of healing and casting out demons. But this would have been the perfect time for Jesus to take the credit if He was using his own intrinsic powers if that were the case.

And when we go through the Gospel accounts we find that at every point without exception what Jesus said is the same!

In Mark 5:1-20 reporting the case of the man with a legion of demons we read (v 19) : "Go home to your people and report to them what great things the Lord has done for you, and how He had mercy on you." Jesus did not say what I, Jesus, have done for you, but what the Lord did. Jesus referred again to the Lord as one other than Himself.

In John 14:10-11 Jesus attributes the miraculous deeds to God rather than Himself: "Do you not believe that I am in the Father, and the Father is in Me? The words that I say to you I do not speak on My own initiative, but the Father abiding in Me does his works. 11. Believe Me that I am in the Father, and the Father is in Me; otherwise believe on account of the works themselves." The reference to "the Father abiding in me does his works" indicates one other than Himself, just as in the preceding passages. Passage after passage state this same truth. It is the biblical teaching concerning the humanity of Christ in his life on earth.

The passage in John 11:1-44 is the most pointed on the part of Jesus concerning this truth. The context of what Jesus says is clear. It is the incident when Jesus raised his friend Lazarus from the dead. Here is what Jesus said about what was to take place (v 4) : "This sickness is not unto death, but for the glory of God, that the Son of God may be glorified by it." The key phrase is "for the glory of God." God's power will be on display through his Son to bring Him glory. The people are to conclude from the glory that was displayed that He was their Messiah who had come. When the time came for the miracle to take place Jesus prayed to God openly in public:

> John 11:41 And Jesus raised his eyes, and said, "Father, I thank Thee that though heardest Me. 42 And I knew that thou hearest Me always; but because of the people standing around I said it, that they may believe that though didst send Me.

Martha previously had said that she knew that "whatever you ask of God" God would do it, and Jesus did not correct her. Jesus attributes the raising of Lazarus to God hearing Him and says that He wanted the people witnessing the miracle to know that He was a man sent by God from it.

That is what He directly says He wanted them to conclude, **not** that He did it by his own personal power and that it indicated He was God in the flesh! That fact that He was indeed God in the flesh would follow as a subsequent conclusion after the Cross and the Resurrection, but not by virtue of the miracle.

Nothing could be clearer from Jesus' own words.

Here is something else that is important. In John 5:36, Jesus says something very similar:

> John 5:36 ". . . the very works that I do, bear witness of Me, that the Father has sent Me."

Jesus declares that the works He did bear witness that the Father sent Him, not that He was God, but a man sent by God.

5. The perfect and sinless Jesus was brought to perfection through living out his life as a man.

We have seen that it is biblical teaching and not a human supposition that Jesus grew in wisdom and knowledge as a boy into manhood, that He was born of a woman under the Law living in complete obedience to it, that He lived as a man in dependence on God, and did his miracles by the power of the Holy Spirit. Now we will see that Jesus' learning and perfecting process did not cease until He cried "it is finished".

How do we know this? We read in Heb 2:10 "For it was fitting for Him, for whom are all things, in bringing many sons to glory, to perfect the author of their salvation through sufferings." We also read in Heb 5:9 "And having been made perfect, He became to all those who obey Him the source of eternal salvation."

We need to look carefully at the word *perfect*. The Greek word *teleioo* translated "to having been made perfect" can be misleading. A better rendering is "Having been *perfected*," as Greek expositors tell us (W.E. Vine, for example). The Greek word means bringing to a goal or proper end by a process. It is used of (1) accomplishing (to finish or fulfill), and of (2) bringing to completeness, of persons. W.E. Vine says "Of Christ's assured completion of his earthly course, in the accomplishment of the Father's will, the successive stages culminating in his death (Luke 2:32; Heb 2:10)." The idea here is not to impugn Christ's deity and inherent perfection, but to show that Scripture says the man Jesus, who was sinless, went all the way to human perfection as a man. And He went all the way to human perfection, not through passive obedience, that is, without breaking any of God's laws, but through active obedience never failing to perform all righteousness while enduring sufferings and being obedient.

In John 19:28-30 the same Greek root is used as in Hebrews 2:10:

> John 19:28 After this, Jesus, knowing that all things had already been accomplished, in order that the Scripture might be fulfilled, said "I am thirsty." 29. A jar of sour wine was standing there; so they put a sponge full of the sour wine upon a branch of hyssop, and brought it up to His mouth. 30. When Jesus therefore had received the sour wine, He said, "It is finished!" And He bowed His head, and gave His spirit.

When Jesus said "it is *finished,"* it meant that all was fulfilled and accomplished, so that He had completed in his life what God required to be a perfect sacrifice and God would be propitiated in his death on the Cross. Jesus had already prayed (John 17:19) "And for their sakes I sanctify Myself, that they themselves also maybe sanctified in truth." But the word *accomplished* in v 28 is from the same Greek root *teleioo* as the word *finished* in v 30. The words all imply that there was a process to the Savior's fulfillment of his mission and that process continued from birth to death. Jesus was perfect at every level of maturity and achievement but had not yet fulfilled all that He needed to fulfill. He was not perfected in that sense until He cried out "it is finished". The Father's words earlier, "This is My Son in whom I am well pleased" was an affirmation of his progress in being perfected.

6. Jesus lived his life on earth by faith and not by sight.

The Bible makes a definitive statement about faith in 2 Cor 5:7:

> 2 Cor 5:7 "For we walk by faith, not by sight."

What does this mean? Faith and sight are polar opposites to each other. When one walks by faith he is not walking by sight, and vice versa, if one is walking by sight it means that it could not be said that he is walking by faith. God wants this truth to be clear in our thinking, that one walks either by faith or by sight.

There is natural faith in human affairs and faith in God. But the principle is the same. In the case of human faith one acts all the time without knowing that what one depends on will not be harmful. We eat food without knowing whether it is poisonous or not. And we trust people that we do not know, trusting that they will not harm us. It is acting on faith without "sight."

But faith in God is not a natural experience. When man died spiritually he lost the natural ability to believe his Maker, and with time God became even more obscure to man. The Apostle Peter understood faith when he said "That the proof of your faith, being more precious than gold which is perishable, even though tested by fire, may be found to result in praise and glory and honor at the revelation of Jesus Christ; and though you have not seen Him, you love Him, and though you do not see Him now, but believe in Him, you greatly rejoice with joy inexpressible and full of glory, obtaining as the outcome of your faith the salvation of your souls" (1 Peter 1:7-9). Scripture is replete with examples of the polarization of faith and sight, especially when it comes to faith in God.

The natural man lives his life by what he perceives in the world around him, or in his own little world. He pays no attention to the words of the one true God who created him. He is infected with original sin and guilt from the curse of God as a result of Adam's sin, and is blinded by the love of his own sin. He does not sense or live in the spiritual world that regenerated believers walk in. Believers may walk sometimes by sight and sometimes by faith or they may walk, some times in the power of the Spirit. They may sometimes be obedient to the word of God, and sometimes walk in their flesh, disobedient to God.

Heb 11:1 says, "Now faith is the assurance of things hoped for, the conviction of things not seen."

Hope means confidence in God for the future. Again faith means this confidence in God and not seeing it, but depending on God for it.

> Rom 8:24 "For in hope we have been saved, but hope that has been seen is not hope; for why does one also hope for what he sees? 25 But if we hope for what we do not see, with perseverance we wait eagerly for it."

So this is what it means to live and walk by faith. In each biblical passage faith is contrasted with seeing or direct knowledge.

Does this apply to Jesus? It is absolutely clear that it was true in Jesus' early life, stated above in the first truth that Jesus was a human who was born, grew, and increased in knowledge and wisdom without the use of divine abilities. At that point in time He certainly walked by faith and not sight as Scripture describes. By faith He waited and hoped for all that was prophesied to come true and studied to know what his part was in fulfilling the law and pleasing God. All the while his convictions were of things not yet seen by Him, or things He could not see by human sight alone. He relied on God through the words of Scripture. But it didn't stop there, because He learned that it was He Himself who was the God-Man and fulfillment of the biblical promises of the Messiah.

Not only is it clear from Jesus' growing in knowledge and wisdom when He was young that He lived by faith. Scripture elsewhere says explicitly Jesus Christ lived his life by faith in God. This is biblical teaching concerning Jesus' life.

The Apostle Peter says (1 Peter 2:23) "And while being reviled, He did not revile in return; while suffering, He uttered no threats, but kept entrusting Himself to Him who judges righteously." The word *entrusting* could as well be translated *committed*. It is the Greek word *paradidomi*. W. E. Vine says it carries the meaning of delivering or entrusting something to someone. This is exactly what Jesus was doing all through his life. He was not trusting in his own strength, but giving everything over to, and entrusting Himself to God his Father, who was judging righteously in every experience of Christ's trials as well as his suffering. It is exactly what we mean by living by faith.

Even more direct we read in Hebrews 2:13 "I will put My trust in Him." Hebrews indicates this as prophetically speaking of our Lord Jesus Christ, of Him living by faith. This is the teaching of Scripture. Matt 27:43 uses the same Greek word for trust *peitho*, used by the chief priests, elders and scribes in derision against Jesus:

> Matt 27:43 He trusts in God; let Him deliver Him now, if He takes pleasure in Him; for He said, "I am the Son of God."

This is all reflected prophetically in Psalm 22:8: "He trusted in the Lord, let Him rescue Him" (NKJV). This is the direct teaching of Scripture that Christ Jesus put his trust in God.

Another clear affirmation of Jesus' faith is made by the writer of Hebrews in Heb 3:2: "He was faithful to Him who appointed Him, as Moses was in all his house." The Holy Spirit makes a comparison between Jesus' faith and Moses' faith. This statement could not have been made if the two men were not living by and being faithful to their commitment to trusting in God. The Greek word for *faithful* in this case is *piston*, from the root *pistos*, meaning **faith**. The verb form of this root, *pistos* is the same word for *to believe* throughout the New Testament.

If we had to pick one passage from Holy Scripture which teaches Jesus, as a true man, lived his life by the power of faith in the one true God and his Word, it would be Hebrews 12:1-3:

> Heb 12: 1 Therefore, since we have so great a cloud of witnesses surrounding us, let us also lay aside every encumbrance, and the sin which so easily entangles us, and let us run with endurance the race that is set before us; 2. fixing our eyes on Jesus, the author and perfecter of faith, who for the joy set before Him endured the cross, despising the shame, and has sat down at the right hand of the thrown of God. 3 For consider Him who has endured such by sinners against Himself, so that you may not grow weary and lose heart.

This makes the comparison here with the good examples of the faith lived by the cloud of witnesses in Hebrews 11 together with us who are trying to live by faith to his Son Jesus. It compares our living by faith as a race, a race we should run with great endurance and without the encumbrances of sin, a race of faith just like Jesus ran as a perfect example except for the sin. That comparison would be impossible to propose to the readers of Hebrews if it was not comparing like things with like. The great cloud of witnesses lived by the faith in the one true God to deliver on the promises He made in his Scriptures, and the writer of Hebrews assures his readers the great cloud of witnesses were justly rewarded just like Jesus was rewarded. These witnesses all lived life by believing things that were unseen as opposed to things that were seen and commonly practiced and accepted by their family and friends as explained in Hebrews 11:1-3.

Examples in Jesus' Life

Not only do we have the explicit teaching of Scripture that Jesus lived by faith, but we can mention events in the ministry of Christ Jesus' life when He was frustrated and disappointed with his followers due to their lack of faith. There are at least ten of them recorded in the gospels: Matt 6:30, 8:26, 14:31, 16:8, 17:20, 21:21; Mark 4:40; Luke 8:25, 12:28, 17:6.

The first example is presented in three different biblical passages in which Jesus displayed faith as an example to his disciples:

(1) He taught faith in God for protection of one's life (Matt 8:23-27, Mark 4:35-41, and Luke 8:22-25).

> Luke 8:22-25 "Now it happened, on a certain day, That He got into a boat with his disciples. And He said to them, "let us cross over to the other side of the lake." And they launched out. 23. But as they sailed He fell asleep. And a windstorm came down on the lake, and they were filling with water, and were in jeopardy. 24. And they came to Him and awoke Him, saying, "Master, master, we are perishing!" Then He arose and rebuked the wind and the raging of the water. And they ceased, and there was a calm. 25. But He said to them, "Where is your faith?" And they were afraid, and marveled, saying to one another, "Who can this be? For He commands even the winds and water, and they obey Him!"

Most people are quick to admit Jesus' humanity in being exhausted and falling asleep, making Him like us that He could be so weary that even the storm didn't arouse Him. But then, when He awoke He is looked at as the omnipotent God to save all of them, making Him then unlike us.

However, the narrative of this event in Jesus' life can be understood as teaching us how He functioned as a man living by faith. Why did Jesus immediately without hesitation admonish his disciples for their lack of faith, if his own calmness were due to his deity? To mix or change modes of operation in the Savior's life in a split second acting from his position of man to acting as God and then back to man again in a split second is not a natural way to interpret this passage of Scripture, which ignores the context of what Jesus said.

An objection could be raised that the disciples should have had faith in Him as God the Son, with power over nature, instead of being afraid. That means He was not admonishing them about not having faith in God the Father, but not having faith in Him personally. This reverses the argument here. But that would be different from what Jesus always taught, faith in God the Father, with no emphasis on trusting Him personally, with one exception where He said that you believe in God, believe also in me, where the context is different.

(2) Jesus taught faith in God to overcome life's anxieties over provisions.

> Matt 6:30: "But if God so arrays the grass of the field, which is alive today and tomorrow is thrown into the furnace, will He not much more do so for you, O men of little faith?" cf. Luke 12:28.

In this context Jesus is talking about wealth and provisions and being anxious for the things of life. He always brought circumstances around to instructing the disciples about faith. Here He talks from his own life experience of not being anxious while owning nothing but trusted in the Father to provide for Him everything He needed. It was an example of living by faith. He had the platform to teach on faith because that's exactly how He was living, affirming his credibility and his humanity.

(3) Jesus taught faith in God by example to increase faith and calm one's fears.

> Matt 14:31: "And immediately Jesus stretched out his hand and took hold of him, and said to him, "O you of little faith, why did you doubt?" cf, Mark 6:45-52; John 6:16-21

61

At Peter's request, Jesus commands Peter to join Him walking on the water, and Peter did walk on the water by faith in God in the power of the Holy Spirit. But then he became afraid, and while sinking he cried out "Lord save me." It might be thought this is a good example of Jesus walking on water displaying his power (divine omnipotence) over the forces of nature. But Jesus again uses the circumstances to teach about faith in God.

(4) Jesus taught faith in God to triumph over demons.

> Matt 17:20 And He said to them, "Because of the littleness of your faith; for truly I say to you, if you have faith as a mustard seed, you shall say to this mountain, 'Move from here to there,' and it shall move; and nothing shall be impossible to you." cf, Mark 9:14-29; Luke 9:37-42.

In this situation Jesus is so disappointed with the lack of faith of the people and especially his disciples that, He just could not hold back, and He laments with frustration in his words: "O unbelieving and perverted generation, how long shall I be with you? How long shall I put up with you? Bring him here to me." He was speaking of the young boy who had the demon and the disciples had just been unsuccessful in casting the demon out. Jesus had previously already told them (and us) how He Himself was able to rebuke a demon and cast him out of a person. He said it was by the Spirit of God or the finger of God (Mathew 12:28, Luke 11:20). If Jesus were acting from his own intrinsic powers as God the Son, He would have told us so, but instead He tells us completely otherwise!

The Lord Himself, in eternity past, was the one who decided that by faith only a man could know God and then live his life in this world to please Him. Heb 11:6 "And without faith it is impossible to please Him." What about that too? Did Jesus please God? He did. Therefore He had to have faith. And let us also not forget what the Bible says in Rom 14:23 "and whatever is not from faith is sin." If Jesus did something that was not from faith, what would we have to conclude? That He sinned, which is impossible! Therefore whatever He did **was** from faith!

7. What Jesus taught He received from God the Father and not from Himself.

Jesus, just as Scripture affirms, worked his signs and wonders in the power not of Himself but through the omnipotence of the Holy Spirit. Just as profound as Jesus working and performing great miracles to the watching crowds was his astounding words which amazed the crowds as well. Never a man spoke like this man, they said. Are we to suppose Jesus studied and grew in wisdom like other men and then preached and spoke omnisciently? What does Scripture say?

> Acts 1:1-2 "The first account I composed, Theophilus, about all that Jesus began to do and to teach, 2 until the day He was taken up, after He had by the Holy Spirit given orders to the apostles whom He had chosen."

Here Luke states that Jesus spoke and gave commandments by the power of the Holy Spirit. There should be no question about the source or power in which Jesus spoke. Jesus Himself affirms this same truth in the following passages:

> John 3:34 For He whom God has sent speaks the words of God; for He gives the Spirit without measure.

> John 7:16 My teaching is not Mine but his who sent Me.

> John 8:26 The things I heard from Him, these things I speak to the world.

> John 8:28 I do nothing on My own initiative, but I speak these things as the Father taught Me.

> John 8:40 But you seek to kill Me, a man who has told you the truth, which I heard from God; this Abraham did not do.

> John 12:49 For I did not speak on My own initiative, but The Father Himself who sent Me has given Me commandment, what to say and what to speak.

> John 14:10 Do you not believe that I am in the Father, and the Father is in Me? The words that I say To you I do not speak on My own initiative, But the Father abiding in Me does his works.

> John 17:8 For the words which Thou gavest Me I have given to them;

The literal rendering for "My own initiative" in John 8:28,

12:49, and 14:10 is "not from myself" or "not out of myself." Jesus repeatedly declares that his words are not his own, but given to Him. If He were speaking using his divine attributes, they **would** be his own. The only conclusion is that He was speaking without the use of those attributes as a man given the words by revelation from God.

The fact that Jesus received his words from God the Father and the Holy Spirit is important for another reason, that He was the promised prophet like Moses. Jesus is Prophet, Priest and King, major categories of Scripture concerning Him being Prophet therefore is significant enough that we will devote a whole later chapter to this.

But for now we need to summarize the significance of the biblical doctrine of this chapter. (1) Jesus grew in wisdom and knowledge as a boy into manhood. This means that those who deny that there was ever a time in which Jesus was limited in his wisdom and knowledge but always had full use of his divine omniscience are in error and positively contradict the biblical teaching concerning Christ's life. (2) Jesus was born of woman under the Law living in complete obedience to it. This means that those who deny that Jesus had to live as a man under the law but only had to be ontologically a true man are in error and positively contradict the biblical teaching concerning Christ's life. (3) Jesus lived as a man in dependence on God. This means that those who assert that Jesus always lived his life as the divine Son of God, God the Son, are in error, denying the dependence and submission that is taught in God's Holy Written Word. (4) Jesus did miracles by the power of the Holy Spirit. This means that those who assert that Jesus always did his miracles by his own divine power are in error and contradict the plain teaching of the Word of God. (5) The perfect and sinless Jesus was brought to perfection through living out his life as a man. This means that those who teach that Jesus by virtue of being the Son of God was always perfect as a man are in error. They confuse the fact of being inherently perfect and inherently without sin as man with the necessity of living out a life to perfection as a man under the law. (6) Jesus lived his life on earth by faith and not by sight. This means that those are in error who think that because Jesus was in fact in his being God, He could not live by faith but by the sight of divine omniscience. An informal poll was taken at a very large Evangelical church in which about 55% or more of the members polled thought that Jesus did not live by faith. (7) What Jesus taught He received from God the Father and not from Himself. This means that those are in error who think that Jesus taught from his own personal authority and divine knowledge.

The biblical doctrine goes beyond the idea that Jesus acted and lived out his life as a man through viewing the overall tenor of his life and examination of many examples. Doctrine is never to be established from examples alone. Whole denominations have made that error. Doctrine is established from the positive teaching and declarations of Scripture. In this chapter those positive teachings and declarations have been the only basis for the statements made in the 7 points given above. This gives a presumption concerning how to interpret Jesus' life, but only a presumption, that everything Jesus did in his life during his state of humiliation are to be explained in terms of living as a man without the use of the divine powers that He actually had. Jesus voluntarily set aside the use of his divine abilities. But that does not mean that He did not have them. The temptation of Jesus in the wilderness illustrates this. In order to try to thwart God's plan, Satan tempted Jesus to use the divine powers that He actually had, but Jesus was true to his mission in deliberately not using them!

4.

REASONABLE QUESTIONS

We have seen that the Jesus of the Bible is God the Son, the Second Person of the Trinity, that He is both fully God and fully Man. Concerning his ministry on earth Scripture states some undeniable truths, including that He was Prophet, fulfilling the promise to Moses of a prophet to come like him. The undeniable truth is that: (1) Jesus grew in wisdom and knowledge as a boy into manhood. (2) Jesus was born of woman under the Law living in complete obedience to it. (3) Jesus lived as a man in dependence on God. (4) Jesus did his miracles by the power of the Holy Spirit. (5) The perfect and sinless Jesus was brought to perfection through living out his life as a man. (6) Jesus lived his life on earth by faith and not by sight. (7) What Jesus taught He received from God the Father and not from Himself.

But there are some passages which on the surface could be construed to teach Christ Jesus used his divine attributes in some of the situations in his life and ministry. Most theologians in the modern era interpret them in this way. Below are listed some of the passages most often cited to indicate that Jesus used his own divine powers to perform a miracle or to know something that a normal man would not be able to do or know. The question is whether the biblical teaching of Chapter 3 is adequate to explain these situations. Those passages need to be examined with that in mind.

1. First Reasonable Question

Luke 7:36-50. In this lengthy passage Jesus dines at a Pharisee's house in which a woman who was a known sinner, later identified in John 11:2 as the sister of Martha and Lazarus, was wetting Jesus' feet with her tears and wiping them with her hair, and anointing his feet with perfumed oil. Jesus was very moved by this open display of faith, love and emotions, then proclaims to her in the hearing of all (v 48) "Your sins have been forgiven." Then he said to her "Your faith has saved you; go in peace (v 50)."

Isn't it true that only God can forgive sins? Isn't Jesus Himself acting as God, and not as man? This really seems to be a weighty objection.

We see Jesus pronouncing forgiveness of sins also in Luke 5:20, Matt 9:2, and Mark 2:5. In Matt 9:6 and Mark 2:10 Jesus says He possesses the authority to forgive sins. The explanation for this scriptural statement can be taken two ways. Christ Jesus knew He was God and it was God who was sinned against and therefore it was his place and his place alone to forgive any sin against Himself. However there is another reason for Christ's having authority on earth to make the claim to an individual that his or her sins are forgiven. While it was his prerogative alone to forgive sin, along with all of his other prerogatives of deity, the Son of God chose not to exercise any of those prerogatives in order to live among men as one of them, as John 1:14 declares. However, God the Father did give all authority to the Son of man while He was on earth because He was mediator: Messiah/Christ, Prophet, Priest, and King and Head of his Church in order to facilitate the plan of salvation.

A few observations are appropriate here before we establish the principle which affirms Jesus' claim as a man for possessing authority to forgive sins.

In every situation in the Bible where Jesus makes the statement "your sins are forgiven," the narrative makes sure that the hearer or reader knows that the cause of the forgiveness is a direct result of their demonstration of real faith in the one true God and his Son. From the Old Testament all the way through the New Testament it is established and taught that godly repentance and believing in the one true God comes through faith, and is followed with the promise of God to forgive their sins. Upon believing and repentance God promises every transgression will be blotted out as far as the east is from the west. When the Son of God became incarnate this procedure did not change. If anyone truly believes, his sins, past, present, and future, will be forgiven. And if that wasn't enough, God will make him or her righteous so He can enjoy them in his presence. All of that is a transaction which is completed in heaven.

In every situation where Jesus pronounces a person's sins are forgiven them, the narrative makes it clear that their sins have been forgiven **already**. In other words the forgiveness has already occurred as was demonstrated by their actions of repentance and faith. **All** of the claims made by Jesus are **past tense**. Jesus is declaring something that has already taken place in heaven. By the work of the Holy Spirit in these individuals' lives God has already saved them and forgiven their sins, and Jesus seeing their display of faith, proclaims to them and to the surrounding crowd that their sins are or have been forgiven. He also explains to them their sins are forgiven due to their faith.

Jesus was given the Spirit without measure including all the gifts and graces which comes along with that filling. There is no way Jesus, Messiah and Prophet, could be mistaken about their display of faith, given his own elevated human abilities of discernment, especially when brought to an elevated level by the filling of the Holy Spirit without measure.

Jesus had and was using perfect human discernment without using divine omniscience, and He would not be fooled into accepting into the kingdom of God even one soul who was not really his own. On certain occasions Jesus did not proclaim to them their sins were forgiven, simply because there was no accompanying evidence of their faith having been demonstrated.

As mentioned above, it is crucial to our understanding that this same phenomenon of forgiving sins on earth in collaboration with the actions of heaven was delegated by Christ to the disciples, and then with their passing, this very same authority falls to the church today.

We submit the following which are the biblical facts to form the doctrine of God's representatives having the authority to declare God's forgiveness of sins upon those who believe and show repentance. And this is to be done in exactly the same way as Jesus did it, except for his perfect discernment.

John 20:22-23 And when He said this, He breathed on them, and said to them, "Receive the Holy Spirit 23 If you forgive the sins of any, their sins have been forgiven them; if you retain the sins of any, they have been retained."

The significant thing to note in this passage is that forgiveness is declared which has already been accomplished. The forgiving and retaining is only a statement on earth of what has already taken place, in the same way that Jesus forgave only those who by faith were already forgiven in heaven.

> Matt 16:19 "I will give you the keys of the kingdom of heaven; and whatever you shall bind on earth shall be bound in heaven, and whatever you shall loose on earth shall be loosed in heaven."

> Matt 18:18 "Truly I say to you, whatever you shall bind on earth shall be bound in heaven; and whatever you shall loose on earth shall be loosed in heaven."

The Lord using slightly different language says virtually the same thing as quoted by John, and extends his authority to bind or loose to his disciples. The tense in the original language, which does not come out in the translations, is that the words *bound* and *loosed* are clearly past tense. It should read "whatever you bind on earth shall have been bound in heaven," and so forth.

If we preach to the hearers of the gospel that God promises to them upon their repentance and belief that they will receive the remission of sins, we must then have the authority to confirm to them upon their confession they have in fact been forgiven of their sins. We must remember that many in the world are burdened with guilt from their many sins, and the Holy Spirit is actively convincing those who are called to repent and believe that they can receive the forgiveness and relief they desperately seek. We are also called upon to inform a sinner to the contrary if in their particular situation they are still in there sins and point out why.

The Bible is replete with sermons promising sinners the remission of sins if they repent and believe.

> Acts 2:37-38 Now when they heard this, they were pierced to the heart, and said to Peter and the rest of the Apostles, "Brethren what shall we do?" 38. And Peter said to them, "Repent and let each of you be baptized in the name of Jesus Christ for the forgiveness of your sins; and you shall receive the gift of the Holy Spirit."

Acts 3:19 Repent therefore and return, that your sins may be wiped away

Forgiveness of sins is initiated in heaven with the calling of an individual to repentance. Faith is issued as a gift from God which includes the forgiveness of sins. Jesus came to preach the gospel to the poor and he established this truth anew. By giving examples of this truth in the presence of his disciples as shown above, he was able to teach in depth this same principle.

It is indeed only God, who forgives sins, and He does it upon repentance and faith, and what Jesus did was only to confirm what the Father had already done.

2. Second Reasonable Question

John 2:23-25 "Now when He was in Jerusalem at the Passover, during the feast, many believed in His name, beholding His signs which He was doing. 24 But Jesus, on His part, was not entrusting Himself to them, for He knew all men, 25 and because He did not need anyone to bear witness concerning man for He Himself knew what was in man."

If, when interpreting this passage, we have a preconceived idea that Jesus did not need to live a complete and entire righteous life as a man, it would be easy to conclude as many have, **"When He was performing his miraculous signs and wonders and teachings, wasn't He fully self-conscious of his omniscience and omnipotence and was at the same time exercising them, except all according to his Father's will?"** The problem is that if Jesus was living his life in any other way than how a normal man would, He could never identify with, or sympathize with our weaknesses as the Scripture very clearly says He did in Heb 5:1 and Heb 4:15:

Heb 5:1: For every high priest taken from among men is appointed on behalf of men in things pertaining to God, in order to offer both gifts and sacrifices for sins; 2 he can deal gently with the ignorant and misguided, since he himself also is beset with weakness;

Heb 4:15 "For we do not have a high priest who can not sympathize with our weaknesses, but one who has been tempted in all things as we are yet with out sin.

To conclude Jesus was not capable to know what was in

70

man's heart and the potential of this particular sin is an insult to Jesus' intelligence and wisdom. Since it was the Father who said He had to be made like us and be tempted like us and suffer and learn obedience like us, it would render the Father's will inconsistent with his word. Jesus learned what the Father's will was by talking to Him in prayer, as do other men of God, or according to Heb 2:17 his brethren did. The passage does not say that Jesus knew what He did by use of his divine abilities. In the incident recorded in John 2:23-25 it would not be difficult for Jesus to exercise discernment as a mature, sinless man. Jesus we must remember was absolutely clear in his thinking and discernment, being sinless and being filled with the Spirit without measure.

In any event, one could never claim with scriptural authority that John 2:23-25 explicitly says Jesus accessed his own divine powers to know what was in the heart of any man. It can only be interpreted that way by conjecture from a preconceived view of his life. Consider Jer 17:9-10:

> Jer 17: 9 The heart is more deceitful than all else and is
> desperately sick; who can understand it? 10 I, the Lord, search
> the heart, I test the mind, even to give to each man according to
> his ways, according to the results of his deeds.

Christ Jesus using his crystal clear human mind enlightened by the Holy Spirit with perfect understanding of this passage in Jeremiah, together with the many references to the condition of man's heart and mind, was able to discern the attitudes of the men not only here in John chapter 2, but in John 8:30-31, and all the way through his ministry. To conclude Jesus used his divine attributes in these situations without any direct statement to that effect would impugn his wisdom and his understanding of his mission.

3. Third Reasonable Question

John 4:4-42 gives us an account of Jesus' meeting a woman of Samaria. He met the woman at the well outside the town. Jesus asked her to call her husband and she responded as follows:

> John 4:17 The woman answered and said "I have no husband."

> Jesus said to her, "you have well said, 'I have no husband'; 18. for you have had five husbands, and the one whom you now have is not your husband; this you have said truly." 19. The woman said to Him, "Sir, I perceive you are a prophet."

Again, as many interpret it, **doesn't this indicate that Jesus was exercising his divine power of omniscience to know the woman's past life?**

But the woman actually perceived correctly, "Sir you are a Prophet." Scripture does indeed declare that Jesus was a prophet, one like Moses. Deut 18:18 "I will raise up a prophet from among their countrymen like you" Since Jesus was a prophet, the details of the woman's life could be revealed to Him in the same way as a human prophet. We can believe that Jesus was fulfilling and performing his office as a prophet of God and was privy to this information concerning the woman's past because it was deemed necessary for Him to know in order to gain this woman's full attention and ultimately the attention of the whole town. This event is without a doubt a classic biblical example of a genuine Spirit-filled prophet at work. There were other occasions in the life of Christ when he knew some details in an event that were not revealed or prophesied in the Old Testament and being a prophet he was privy to them just like other prophets before him and after him. And in the New Testament the same is true. Peter and Paul would be two of many good biblical examples.

4. Fourth Reasonable Question

Mark 5:25-34, Matt 9:20-22, Luke 8:43-48. Here we have the incident involving the woman with the issue of blood. Consider the words that raise a question.

> Matt 9:20-22 And suddenly, a woman who had a flow of blood for twelve years came from behind and touched the hem of His garment. 21. For she said to herself, "if only I could touch the hem of His garment I shall be made well. 22. But Jesus turned around, and when He saw her He said, "Be of good cheer, daughter; your faith has made you well." And the woman was made well from that hour.

> Mark 5:30 And Jesus, immediately knowing in Himself that power had gone out of Him, Turned around in the crowd and said, "Who touched my clothes?"

It is a reasonable question to ask, **"Isn't this a clear example of Jesus' exercise of his own divine powers?"**

First of all, in each of the three recorded versions of this event in the life of Christ Jesus, He declares to all and especially to the woman with the infirmity, it was her faith that healed her or made her well. Second, the Greek word for Jesus knowing is *epiginomai*, which taken in its proper sense means experiential knowledge, that He became aware of the fact. Note this healing miracle was not premeditated as the narrative says; it happened without his initiating it. Jesus who possessed all divine attributes was made aware of power going out from him. It wasn't a matter of Him deliberately exercising his divine power. We are shown at the mount of transfiguration that Jesus was still in possession of all of the divine attributes but had just temporarily laid aside the use of them. To conclude Jesus called upon his supernatural powers in this instance would be to misunderstand not only the nature of the faith this woman possessed, but to misjudge what happened. Not only did Jesus not call upon his own powers but he didn't even have his Father's permission to use them. As far as Him not knowing who touched the hem of his garment, Jesus was not just "playing to the crowd." It was not that He knew all along and asked a disingenuous question. He asked because He was surprised the miracle occurred and genuinely wanted to know to whom in the crowd this great faith belonged. We must conclude Jesus was ignorant of or without knowledge of this miracle until it involuntarily took place. Here is an instance of the Holy Spirit performing a miraculous healing in their midst, even to the surprise of the Savior Himself. This event is here listed as a possible objection to the biblical doctrine of Christ's humanity but it could have been used to further reinforce the fact He was not exercising his divine attributes at all. What we actually see is the opposite of Jesus exercising on his own part his divine powers.

5. Fifth Reasonable Question

Didn't performing miracles, overcoming the powers of nature, and so forth, indicate Jesus' deity?

But prophets in the Old Testament, such as Moses and Elijah did miracles that cannot in any way be explained in terms of nature, yet they did not indicate deity belonging to them! So performing miracles contrary to nature does not in itself indicate deity. Therefore there is no way that the miracles of Jesus necessarily show anything more than that Jesus was a prophet like them.

Jesus walked on water, changed water into wine, and calmed the storm. Moses parted the sea, and turned the Nile River into blood. Moses told Aaron to turn the rest of Egypt's waters to blood. These miracles all indicated there was a prophet of God working in the power of God present. Nothing more.

But it was necessary for Jesus to prove he was a prophet in order to fulfill Scripture! The fact that Jesus was approved of God as a prophet, the Prophet that had been foretold and fulfilled Messianic prophecies, including that the Messiah would be God, indicates his deity.

So the supposition that the miracles show Jesus' deity, indicating that He used his own inherent divine powers, does not appear to be a valid question after all.

6. Sixth Reasonable Question

What about details not given in the Old Testament prophecies that Jesus had knowledge of? Does that not show that Jesus relied on his divine omniscience? The answer is, No. We must not forget that Jesus was also prophet and could prophesy details concerning what would happen in his own life. This would be by divine revelation to Him as a man, and not by virtue of his divine abilities. Again that is through the Holy Spirit. And, of course, being a prophet, He could receive new revelation.

Moses also received a large amount of new revelation. Who could possibly know that God made the world in six days, or that He in fact even made the world, and especially from nothing. We know God made the world from nothing but He formed man from the dust of the world. How about the fall of man? That information is right up there in importance with the revelation we received from Jesus.

74

7. Seventh Reasonable Question.

John 1:45 Philip found Nathanael and said to him, "we have found Him of whom Moses in the law and also the prophets wrote, Jesus of Nazareth, the son of Joseph." 46. And Nathanael said to him, "can any good thing come out of Nazareth?" Philip said to him, "Come and see." 47. Jesus saw Nathanael coming to Him, and said of him, "Behold an Israelite indeed, in whom is no guile!" 48. Nathanael said to Him, "How do you know me?" Jesus answered and said to him, "Before Philip called you, when you were under the fig tree, I saw you."

Doesn't Jesus' knowing details that an ordinary man would not know indicate the use of his divine powers?

There are too many different opinions attached to this event in our Lord's life to begin to list all of them, but following are the most popular: Jesus was omnipresent or everywhere present, so he was with Nathanael under the fig tree. Jesus was omniscient so he knew Nathanael's heart and mind so Jesus saw him in his mind and knew everything in that way. Jesus was capable of supersonic travel, kind of like coming into a room and passing through the doors or walls, or like when after his resurrection and walking along the road he could just appear or disappear from their sight.

To conclude any of those explanations are true one must first believe and be moved by the presupposition that Christ walked the roads and villages during his ministry not by faith and all his divine attributes available to him were functioning even with or without his Father's permission. There is nothing stated in the narrative to substantiate this opinion. Scripture is void of any details leading to that conclusion.

The natural or normal sense of this narrative is to allow Jesus the opportunity to function in his office as prophet and he would be given any pertinent information he might need all provided by the Holy Spirit. It is even possible that Jesus spotted Nathanael unawares under the fig tree doing something which would cause Jesus to conclude Nathanael to be a true devout Israelite. The Greek word for guile *dolos* means deceit or trickery or fraud etc. We are not given any further details and we do not need to supply any additional details from our own imagination. Jesus knew many, many things as an ordinary man that are not recorded in Scripture. There may have been other reports that Jesus heard about Nathanael before meeting him personally which would identify him as a true Israelite, and Nathanael be pointed out under the fig tree, in humble worship of God without pretensions, confirming the reports, and all the very first time Jesus saw him. This is a plausible interpretation, without the necessity of assuming that Jesus used divine powers.

8. Eighth Reasonable Question

> John 10:17-18 "For this reason the Father loves Me, I lay down My life that I may take it again. No one has taken it away from Me, but I lay it down on my own initiative; I have authority to lay it down, and I have authority to take it up again. This commandment I received from my Father."

Doesn't Jesus here say explicitly that He has the right to lay down his life and take it up again on his own personal initiative, raising Himself from the dead by his own power, which only God can do? And doesn't that mean Jesus would use his own divine power, exercising his attribute of omnipotence?

It certainly sounds like Jesus is acting and speaking from his own divine nature. If you read this passage with a preconceived view, it would be easy to draw that conclusion.

Three points will help to persuade the reader of the truth of the above passage:

(1) There is no argument or contradiction in Jesus' words that He has the power to lay down his life. He is God and by faith He knows He is God and this vital fact that He **is** God is explicitly taught in Scripture. But if He did not lay down his life the plan of God would have been thwarted, and we would still be spiritually dead in our sins. So Jesus' mission was to fulfill the plan of God's reconciliatory work which required Him to be a man and live as a true man fulfilling the law in our place. Yes, He had this power, but according to Heb 9:14, He was the one "who through the eternal Spirit offered Himself without blemish to God." The Spirit did the actual offering.

76

(2) The next part of this passage seems to be very confusing to most interpreters. It ought to be far from confusing. Of course Jesus could have raised Himself from the dead, but if He did that would prove that He was not truly dead or else not a true man. Dead men do not do anything; much less raise themselves from death. On the other hand, He could raise Himself if He were not truly man and God indissolubly joined in the God-Man, something that from chapter 2 we know is impossible. Moreover, it was the Father who raised his Son from the dead through the Holy Spirit as the Scriptures so explicitly tell us. So the explanation must be other than Jesus actually raised Himself.

(3) Jesus says in this passage "For this reason the father loves Me." This is an important confession by Jesus, telling us, while He had authority as God the Son to die and raise in his own divine power, He did not do these things on his own human initiative but rather remained obedient to the Father's will and not his own. And this is the reason his Father loves Him. Jesus said "I always do those things which please Him."

So what is the correct explanation? Jesus voluntarily laid his life down as a man, by his own initiative allowing men to crucify Him. And that was because God gave Him that right as a man. But when He laid his life down, the time of his state of humiliation was over! He now had the right by his own divine power to raise Himself. However, He did not do that, though He had the right. Instead, He waited upon the Father and Spirit to raise Him. Jesus' words are correct and do not contradict other statements of Scripture that seem to indicate something to the contrary.

9. Ninth Reasonable Question

Another reasonable question relates to a supposed difference between Jesus and his apostles when they performed miracles. **Don't we have to suppose that because the apostles were mere men that they performed miracles by a different power from the Lord Jesus Christ who was not a mere man?**

To answer this question we need to examine at least a few of the incidents involving ordinary men performing miracles to draw a comparison with Jesus' ministry.

(1) First Miracle Example

Beginning with the Apostle Peter, after Peter saw Jesus walking on the water he called out to Jesus:

> Matt 14:28 And Peter answered Him and said, "Lord, if it is You, command me to come to You on the water." 29 So He said, "Come." And when Peter had come down out of the boat, he walked on the water to go to Jesus. But when he saw that the wind was boisterous, he was afraid; and beginning to sink he cried out, saying, "Lord, save me!" 31 And immediately Jesus stretched out his hand and caught him, and said to him, "O you of little faith, Why did you doubt?"

This episode shows Peter like his Master had control over the natural laws of science. But just like Jesus, who was a man, it had to be done in the power of the Holy Spirit accessed only by faith in the power of the Holy Spirit, since only God has the power to alter the forces of nature. This is borne out by Jesus' words to Peter "O you of little faith." Peter knew he did not have this kind of power in himself and to think otherwise would be wrong. Peter was taught by Jesus how to access God's miraculous power and we see it in the next example, in which Peter was also involved.

Looking at Peter again, in Acts 5:1-10.

> Acts 5:1 But a certain man Ananias, with Sapphira his wife, sold a possession. 2 And he kept back part of the proceeds, his wife being aware of it, and brought a certain part and laid it at the Apostles' feet. 3 But Peter said, "Ananias, why has Satan filled your heart to lie to the Holy Spirit and keep back part of the price of the land for your self? 4 While it remained, was it not your own? And after it was sold, was it not in your own control? Why have you conceived this thing in your heart? You have not lied to men but to God." 5 Then Ananias, hearing these words, fell down and breathed his last. So great fear came upon all those who heard these things. 6 And the young men arose and wrapped him up, carried him out and buried him. 7 Now it was about three hours later when his wife came in, not knowing what had happened. 8 And Peter answered her, "Tell me whether you sold the land for so much?" She said "Yes, for so much." 9 Then Peter said to her, "How is it that you have agreed together to test the Spirit of the Lord? Look, the feet of those who have buried your husband are at the door, and will carry you out." 10 Then immediately she fell down at his feet and breathed her last. And

the young men came in and found her dead, and carrying her out, buried her by her husband.

On this occasion the Apostle Peter at first sight seems to have omniscience, but no thinking student of the Word would even suggest Peter to be omniscient. Peter in the will of God was told by the Holy Spirit everything he needed to know about what was going on in the minds of Ananias and Sapphira. And Peter being in authority and the leader of the church using the information he received from God knew exactly what would happen and exactly what he should do. But there is no difference between what Peter did and what Jesus did with the woman at the well in Samaria.

(2) Second Miracle Example

Peter again appears in a miracle. We see a disciple named Tabitha in Acts 9:36-43, Dorcas in Greek, a woman abounding with deeds of kindness and charity, which she did continually. She fell sick and died, and they washed her body and they laid it in an upper room. Peter came and sent the mourners out of the room, knelt down and prayed. Then turning to the body, he said, "Tabitha, arise." And she opened her eyes, and when she saw Peter, she sat up. He took her by the hand and raised her up and called the mourners and presented her alive.

Again, no one would ever believe Peter a mere man could raise the dead. Yet what Peter did was no different from what Jesus did in raising the dead daughter of Jairus.

(3) Third Miracle Example

The first martyr of the church after Jesus' ascension was Stephen.

> Acts 6:8 And Stephen, full of grace and power, was performing great wonders and signs among the people.

Like Jesus, the great wonders and signs he was performing were to affirm and authenticate the message from God. The words of his sermon were so potent they murdered him. And like Jesus, Stephen preached in the power of the Holy Spirit and not in his own power.

(4) Fourth Miracle Example

Saul, the man who became the beloved Apostle Paul, approved of putting Stephen to death at the time that occurred, but was later saved in a miraculous way on the Damascus road. He performed many miracles, signs, and wonders just like Jesus did all by the power of God the Spirit.

> Acts 19:10 And this took place for two years, so that all who lived in Asia heard the word of the Lord, both Jews and Greeks. 11 And God was performing extraordinary miracles by the hands of Paul, 12 so that handkerchiefs or aprons were even carried from his body to the sick, and the diseases left them and the evil spirits went out.

The length of Paul's ministry exceeded that of Jesus, and we must admit that what Paul did is very impressive. But Scripture states that all was done in the name of the risen Jesus or in the power of God.

In terms of the variety and kinds of miracles that the Apostles did was the same as what Jesus did and were attributed to the same Spirit of God that Jesus' miracles were attributed to. There is no indication of any difference. They were mere men, yet the miracles were the same.

10. Tenth Reasonable Question

A reasonable question that might be asked is, **"Doesn't all of what is being said seems to deprecate the incarnation, as though the divine nature is moot or inapplicable to the God-Man"? Jesus living without the use of his divine powers seems to deny the incarnation itself. It makes the profession of being both fully God and fully man empty, just lip-service.**

The answer is, No. The exaltation of Christ after the resurrection proves that there is nothing inherent in the incarnation that excludes Jesus' divine authority or use of his divine powers. This is very important. It is not the incarnation that explains Jesus not using divine powers inherent to Himself. The nonuse of his real and inherent divine powers was a completely voluntary choice on the part of God the Son as the eternal divine God.

Conclusion

In this chapter it is found that there are adequate interpretations to the contrary for all of the cases where it is supposed that there were exceptions to Jesus acting only as a man. These explanations show that these cases do not **necessarily** require that conclusion. Rather these interpretations that we have given are consistent with the overwhelming teaching of Scripture concerning Jesus' life. In later chapters we will find there is a solid biblical reason for the conclusion that Jesus **always** acted without the use of his inalienable inherent powers.

At the end of Chapter 3 we considered the presumption of the biblical doctrine of Christ's life on earth. In the history of the Christian Church only the heretical Kenoticists followed the biblical doctrine of Christ's life as a presumption in understanding the events in Jesus' life. But they did it from false premises and a rationalistic stance. They rejected Chalcedon in the process, confusing the very essence of the incarnation with the voluntary self-emptying of Jesus' use of his powers. The very best Christian expositors almost invariably interpret the events in terms of Jesus' deity even to this day.

5.

CHRIST'S HUMILIATION AND EXALTATION

Christ's Humiliation

We have already examined the doctrine of Scripture concerning Christ's humanity, the fact that everything in his life on earth prior to his resurrection can be explained as living in the power of the Holy Spirit and not his own power. Now we will discover that Scripture gives an explanation for this. It is the doctrine of Christ's Kenosis.

The term *Kenosis* is taken from the Greek text of Phil 2:7 where the Greek word *ekenosen* is used. The word *ekenosen* in English has the meaning of "emptied." This chapter has been entitled "Christ's Humilation and Exaltation." The Kenosis should indicate something more to us than mere humiliation as we will see.

The kenosis passage of Philippians 2, as it appears in the KJV translation is:

5 Let this mind be in you, which was also in Christ Jesus: 6 Who, being in the form of God, thought it not robbery to be equal with God: 7 But made himself of no reputation, and took upon him the form of a servant, and was made in the likeness of men: 8 And being found in fashion as a man, he humbled himself, and became obedient unto death, even the death of the cross.

Here we cite the passage from the NASB, another translation and include the significant original Greek words involved. The Apostle Paul writes under the inspiration of the Holy Spirit:

5. "Have this attitude in your selves which was also in Christ Jesus, 6 who although He existed [*huparchon*] in the form [*morphe*] of God, did not regard equality [*isa*] with God a thing to be grasped [*harpagmos*], 7 but emptied [*ekenosen*] Himself, taking [*lambon*] the form [*morphe*] of a bond-servant [*doulous*], and being made [*ginomai*] in the likeness [*homoiomati*] of men. 8 and being found in appearance [*schema*] as a man, He humbled Himself by

82

becoming obedient to the point of death, even death on a cross."

Philippians chapter 2 tells us of Christ being our example to follow by humbling Himself. The word *empty* is translated various ways. In the KJV it is translated "made of no reputation." This is an interpretation rather than a translation according to usage in the Greek language. But it gives the proper example for believers to follow. To understand how this passage contributes to our understanding of what Christ did, we need to understand what is meant by the words here in verses 6 and 7. The thought that Christ emptied Himself is a very important thought. We have emphasized all along that in Christ's incarnation nothing was lost of the deity of God the Son in becoming a true man. This passage tells us of what Christ voluntarily chose to do when He became man. He chose to act in such a way that He would be a perfect example for us for our attitude in being humble. There can be no thought of Him changing from being truly God, but only of what He would voluntarily give up in the use of his inalienable inherent powers.

The words of Phil 2:5-8 did have a specific meaning to those who were the recipients of the apostle's epistle. Paul wrote to the local church in Philippi who he addresses as saints and who were dear to him, but had fallen prey to serving themselves and their own comfort and honor, thinking on their own things instead of concerning themselves with the welfare of their fellow brothers and sisters in Christ. Paul uses Jesus' life as the example for the Philippians to follow and to correct the situation in Philippi. While dealing with this, Paul under inspiration of the Holy Spirit testifies how Jesus lived his life as the God-Man, affirming that He did so in harmony with both his deity and his humanity. Thus He gave the church very practical instructions to implement in theirs and our lives while at the same time He has made known to us the mode or form the God-Man chose to conduct Himself all of his days on earth. The overriding lesson here, which we will keep in mind throughout our study, is the right example of attitude. Nevertheless it also teaches us something about the life of Jesus in his period of humiliation.

The passage says Christ existed in the form of God and in v 7 He emptied Himself. But just what did He empty Himself of? Scripture says here without any question that He **did** empty Himself. Scripture elsewhere says He did so according to his Father's will.

The Greek word *ekenosen* where it is translated He emptied Himself in Phil 2:7 is used in its root form five times in the New Testament and at least two in the Septuagint – the translation of the Old Testament into Greek. Each time it is used it can be seen to mean basically the same thing, "to empty."

Paul is the only writer to use it in the New Testament. It is first used in Rom 4:14 in the sense to make void or empty. In 1 Cor 1:17 it is to make void or no effect. Also in 1 Cor 9:15 it is to make empty, or void, and then in 2 Cor 9:3 again to make empty or vain. The last time Paul uses it is in the kenosis passage found in Phil 2:5-8, and once again there is no reason to take it in any other sense than the common one of to empty.

In Greek, usage bears this out. The Greek verb *kenoo* used here has the usages, "to empty" a vessel, or "drain"; "to forsake, desert"; or passively, "to be deserted"; "to make of no effect." The associated word *kenos* is used to mean "empty," "exhausted," "fruitless." In combined form *keno-* is used in words translated "depeopled," "empty-boasting," "vain-glorious," "toothless," "empty-minded," "empty-speaking," or "idle talk." In connection with people *kenoo* in Classical and Koine Greek means "to deprive of prerogatives, privileges and possessions." It can also mean to "show an argument to be without foundation." Also, Greek *ekenosen* cannot be understood to mean partial emptying or intermittent emptying, it just means to empty. And *ekenosen* is stronger than to remove one's reputation. All of this comes from standard Lexicons (such as, Liddel & Scott, Kittle, and others).

In the Philippians 2 passage it is true God the Son emptied Himself of his rightful divine prerogatives. That is the thought. The important thing to note here is that there is no justification for taking it to mean that in coming down as a man Christ emptied Himself of his deity, but only temporarily his divine prerogatives. And this is in line with historical usage in the Greek language itself, which was chosen by the Holy Spirit to express the truth concerning God the Son coming down to earth for our redemption.

We must emphasize again it is not only possible to acquire the same attitude as the divine preincarnate Son of God and the man He became, but we are commanded to have this attitude! But it clearly is not possible for us to give up prerogatives or qualities of the living God that we do not even have. That is not the comparison. It is taking on the same kind of position that the God-Man took on, humble submission to God the Father. Only that is to be sought by us.

We need to see that the Greek words included in the text above indicate that being or existing in the form of God means He not only was in possession of the divine attributes, but they were the full representation of his divine nature. We know that God is of one essence with three distinctions and each distinction derives from that one essence. No one distinction is more or less important than the others, since the three are the full expression of God. The Son and the Father are one, and they are one in spiritual substance, all equal and all deriving from one source, God. Christ existed in that form of God and that is the subject of v 6.

At this point we need to examine the other important Greek word *morphe* translated "form" more carefully. In English this word can be confusing. There are two words that could be translated "form" in English, *morphe* and *schema*. It is the latter that most often comes to mind. The word *schema* used v 8, means outward appearance apart from the content of something. A painting or sketch shows the outward appearance but is not a manifestation of the real object. In Greek the word *schema* is even used in cases where there is deception or a false appearance. The word *morphe*, however, indicates something really there not merely in outward appearance but manifested of what is real by what is seen. An example is the English word taken from the Greek, *metamorphosis*. This is a change of form, such as

85

from the larva, to the pupa, to the adult butterfly. The outward appearance is different but there is the same inner biological entity and reality. There is a change in form, but not a change in essence. *Morphe* can indicate a change in outward appearance without change of the inner reality. At the same time, *morphe* in itself is not the inner reality, but the manifestation of it. *Morphe* presupposes a particular nature but does not mean the nature itself, only a necessary manifestation of it. It is like metamorphosis. The inner biological entity is not to be confused with the form, larva, pupa, or butterfly, which are different forms of one essence. Jesus during his life on earth did not manifest the form of God. Even in the Transfiguration, what was manifested of his glory was the true glory of the God-man, where a glimpse of Him beyond the state of his humiliation was seen.

So *morphe* demonstrates something about the reality without it referring to the essence of the thing. In 1 Cor 11:14 as in Gal 4:8 "However at that time, when you did not know God, you were slaves to those which by nature are no gods." The Greek words *ousia* ("being or essence") and *phusis* ("nature") are similar in meaning but the two of these are very far apart in meaning from the word *morphe*, and should never be used interchangeably with it.

What was on display in his preincarnate state was all of the attributes which, when exercised, are the outward expression of his person or essence. And that was his *morphe*. In other words, his attributes were being fully displayed or exercised as the one who He is, God of very God, who acts. And that is what is being stated in Philippians. He emptied Himself of that manifestation or display, that *morphe*. So we understand from v 6 that Christ Jesus was in possession of all of the divine attributes which are the expression or the form of God's nature, and that they were all being exercised in his preincarnate state. And that Christ was of the same nature as God is explicitly affirmed by the next statement in v 6, that He was equal to God. But God the Son did not think that his eternal status and manifestation of his divine nature or form was something He needed to hold on to. And that is proved when in v 7

Scripture says He emptied Himself of the form of God and therefore by extension the manifestation of equality with God. Again He emptied Himself of the form of God, meaning not his divine attributes, but of the outward display or the exercise of the divine attributes that He retained.

So in this act of divine love and humiliation was Jesus made inferior to God in his being or his nature during his humiliation? Absolutely not. Christ was never inferior to God in his nature or essence precisely because He is God. But was He inferior or less than God in the particular role He took in the plan of God? Yes. Just as the apostle says in verse 6, He would voluntarily accept as a reality being less than who He actually was in his function and manifestation. He made the deliberate decision to follow his Father's initiative resulting in Him being made lower than God in his life lived out in a state of humiliation. His Father's initiative became the collective will of God, coming from the Trinity.

This Philippians passage has been seriously misunderstood. It is not primarily about the incarnation of God the Son, but primarily about the mind that the preincarnate God the Son had, as is stated directly in the passage, and requires that the content be understood of the attitude of mind.

This is serious because it otherwise obscures the true meaning of the kenosis and leads to inherent contradictions. The error comes about through misunderstanding the word *morphe*. This is so serious that it is necessary to engage in a polemical refutation of the erroneous way the word is taken and explain the consequences. Here we have given the true meaning, which ought to be clear and simple, but now afterward refute the error.

The erroneous meaning assigned to *morphe* is that it refers to the essential abiding nature of something. *Morphe* has everything to do with a manifestation of a real thing that exists. It presupposes an inner essential abiding nature, but is **not** itself that nature. But this mistake can be so ingrained that other words in the passage also become misrepresented. V 6 refers to **being** in the *morphe* of God, and that is taken to refer to the essence of the preincarnate Christ. But this is not even grammatical. The mere word *being* can refer for example to something that is a mere appearance. One can speak of what one sees as "being" a shadow and not something real using the very same word. So saying that the word *being* always refers to essence is a blunder. *Being* as such can even refer to an imaginary being.

Next, concerning the word *morphe*, biblical usage is supposed to support the idea that it means "the essential abiding nature of something." Rom 8:29, 2 Cor 3:18, Gal 4:19, Phil 3:10 and Rom 12:2 are all supposed to support this meaning. But in order to get that out of these passages they have to be seriously misinterpreted as well. This is not a minor matter, so we have to examine the claims. Though the true meaning has already been given and is transparent, the argument to the contrary must be dealt with. The whole true meaning of the Philippians passage depends on it.

Rom 8:29, "Whom He foreknew, them He predestinated to be conformed to the image of His Son." Here *morphe* in the word *conformed* occurs, supposedly indicating that those in the chain of what God does from foreknowing them to glorifying them are changed in their inner nature, referring to the new nature that takes place by new birth. Believers are changed alright, but not in this way. At regeneration we are **not** changed into the image of Christ. And that is proved by the next passages in the list, which clearly asserts that Christ's own are not yet in the image of Christ!

Christ is the very image of God. So if we are changed into that as an inherent essence, it follows that it is asserting we become divine gods. Rather than that, *morphe* indicates a manifestation of the reality of being regenerated, not being changed to have the divine nature of Christ.

2 Cor 3:18, "As we look on the glory of the Lord we are transformed into His image." Here is a change in *morphe* again. But it does not refer to our essential inner nature! It refers to what we will come to manifest due to the fact that we have been fundamentally changed. It is not the new nature itself. In fact, asserting that it refers to the fundamental change in nature is a denial of the new nature of believers and that they have already been made new creations as believers. It is a serious mistake, all based on an

erroneous meaning for the word *morphe*.

Gal 4:19, Paul says, "My little children, I have birth pains until Christ be formed in you." It is the verb form of *morphe*. But this does not mean the essential inner nature is to be created in believers. It is referring to becoming a true manifest representation of what they really are already.

Phil 3:10 "That I may gain Christ and become conformed unto His death." This does not say that Paul's inner nature is being changed, as supposed, but that He wants to become a true manifest representation of Christ.

Romans 12:2: "Stop being fashioned according to this world, but be transformed in your inner man through the renewing of your mind." Here we have *schema* and *morphe* in the same verse, contrasted with one another. The Greek *schema* is taken to mean what is external and *morphe* what is internal. No, *schema* does refer to what is external even when it looks different from reality, but *morphe* also refers to what is externally manifest, but never when different from what is real. Inner man in Rom 12:2 does not refer to the new nature that all true believers have. The inner man here is something in a person who is a Christian that changes by being renewed in his mind. If by transformation in the inner man it meant the new creation, it would mean that the new creation is impermanent and fluctuates. That contradicts fundamental doctrine about the nature of regeneration. What Christians are to do is not to change their "essential abiding nature," but change the inner man to correspond to the "essential abiding nature" that they have by the new birth.

None of the passages support the idea that *morphe* means the "essential abiding nature" of Christ. But when it is taken this way, the rest of the passage becomes misinterpreted as well.

Not considering his equality with God becomes a statement about his essential divine nature, rather than the glory that He had with the Father before He came into the world. It misses the whole point being made. And then there is a really serious problem with what He emptied Himself of, because if the preceding verse only refers to Christ's "essential abiding nature," the emptying or kenosis **has** to refer to that! And that is heretical. But that is where it takes it!

So we have to insist on the correct meaning of *morphe*, that by *morphe* is meant a true representation and manifestation of something, rather than what is merely and only seen but may be false.

We are now ready to look at the second phrase of verse 7, "taking the form of a bond-servant." The word in the original language does not indicate the idea of being a "bond servant" the way it is given to us in the Old Testament Scripture. There it referred to a person who voluntarily became a permanent servant of another person. In Greek, the word is *doulos*, which simply means **slave**, nothing more or less. To be a slave in those days was not to have any say in your own life and you didn't even belong to yourself. Scripture says Christ took to Himself something. To take to one's self, *lambon,* means to receive into and become a part of and be influenced by. But exactly what did Christ take into Himself? The Greek word *morphe* tells us explicitly what He appropriated, the form of a slave. His position was as a slave indicating what was inherent to Him in the way He came! He manifested that He had no inherent rights! That is in contrast to the position of glory that He had before the incarnation, indicating his form then. But observe that He did not appear as a slave to men around him! Yet his life was not his own, but totally subject to another, God the Father. He was a man in the form of a slave, having that position. But it was a slave to God. This is of the greatest significance, because it tells us again in yet another way that in the state of his humiliation our Lord Jesus Christ did not do anything of his own initiative by his own inherent divine abilities.

Here again the meaning of *morphe* has to be correct and not mean "essential abiding nature." If it means that, the expression doesn't even make any sense, because there is no real existence of anything that is a slave. The real essential abiding nature of one who is a slave is that he is human. But there **can** be an expression of being human as one of the forms of being human. So *morphe* as "essential abiding nature" doesn't fit. There is no separate "inner essential abiding nature of something" that can be called a slave.

The next phrase in verse 7 "being made in the likeness of men" *homoioma* reaffirms that no one observing Him could see anything different or other than humanity emanating from Him. He had no halo and He didn't hover above the ground when He walked. He ate, drank, walked, slept, spoke, and became weary, showed anger, frustration, wept, prayed, was courageous in the face of danger, showed compassion, was faithful to God, and honored his mother, and so forth. But the words here indicate without any doubt that He was a man ontologically.

Next we see in v 8 that Christ was found in fashion or appearance (*schema*) as a man. "Men saw in Christ a human form, bearing, language, action, mode of life ... in general the state and relations of a human being, so that in the entire mode of his appearance made Himself known and was recognized as a man" (Gifford). He did not look like any special person outwardly. His *schema* was not indicating something about his nature, but what people saw.

He acted like a man without any accompanying outward signs of divinity such as we see in the book of Revelation in the state of his exaltation. We reiterate what was said previously, that the signs and wonders He performed were not to prove his deity, but to authenticate that the message He was proclaiming was from God, that He was sent by God. But, of course, all of that should have led them to conclude that He was the Messiah/Christ, and by extension knowing that they should have concluded that He was God in the flesh, "God with us." All that He did should lead logically to that as a conclusion.

V 8 "And being found in appearance as a man, He humbled Himself by becoming obedient to the point of death, even death on a cross." Again the Greek word appearance *schema* is similar to likeness *homoioma* in that in every respect He was found in fashion in every manner of life, actions and humanity in general as observed by his peers to be just like themselves. The Holy Spirit in Scripture drives this point home to us, that Jesus' life was not dominated by his deity and that everything He did could be explained by his humanity.

Three things are mentioned: that he was a slave, a man, and looked like one in every respect. Form indicates the first; likeness indicates the second; fashion indicates the third. All three are necessary to get the whole picture. Expositors tend to deny the first and the third.

As we read through the four Gospels, which are the story of his life on earth, with the proper perspective of his person we should not allow his deity to be extolled to the point of obscuring his humanity.

When the Holy Spirit says the Lord Jesus became obedient even to the point of death, in the last phrase of v 8, He is not referring to duration of time or point in time. The primary sense is that He held out and continued in the face of the most horrible death. It was not only what men could do to Him, but what his Father required from Him in order to satisfy divine justice. The kenosis passage illustrates Christ's attitude of humility as our example and has given us an inside view of the plan of God and how it was accomplished, namely, by emptying Himself of the exercise of any privilege of deity so that He could fulfill what was required of Him to redeem fallen men.

Here we believe is the correct understanding of what is said, which can be supported by looking at the precise meaning that the Greek words have to have in the original biblical text:

1. We are admonished to have the same attitude of submission as Christ.

2. Christ existed in the form of God as God's equal in every respect.

3. He condescended for a period of time to become less than God's equal in function.

4. He emptied Himself of the form of God, referring to his function only, or the exercise of his divine communicable and noncommunicable attributes.

5. He took into Himself the lowest form of a man, a slave.

6. He was made in the likeness of man, with every human attribute and limitation.

7. He was observed outwardly by his peers in every respect as a man.

8. From being Almighty God He became an obedient slave.

9. Christ who was previously only spirit, took on flesh and became the God-Man.

10. Christ's incarnation is permanent.

Christ's Exaltation

In order to complete the kenosis passage of Philippians we must look at 2:9-11 which gives the exaltation of Christ.

In v 5-8 we see the attitude of Christ in his condescension and humiliation in becoming a man and how He lived among men in order to fulfill God's plan and save those who were destined to be saved. In v 9-11 we see the results of his being obedient, even to the point of death and fulfilling all righteousness in order to do so.

In the King James Version we have:

Phil 2:9 Wherefore [*dio*] <1352> God also hath highly exalted [*huperupsosen*] <5251> him, and given [*echarisato*] <5483> (5662) him a name [*onoma*] <3686> which is above [huper] <5228> every name: 10 That [*hina*] <2443> at the name of Jesus [*Iesou*] <2424> every knee should bow, of things in heaven, and things in earth, and things under the earth; 11 And that every tongue should confess [*exomologesetai*] <1843> (5672) that Jesus Christ is Lord [*kurios*] <2962> to the glory [*doxan*] <1391> of God the Father.

Phil 2:9-11 speaks about the exaltation of Jesus Christ. It is God's response to Christ's humiliation. Christ Jesus existed in the form of God but did not regard equality with God a thing to be grasped, but emptied Himself taking the form of a bondservant, a slave, and being made in the likeness of men, and being found in appearance as a man He humbled Himself by becoming obedient to the point of death, even death on a cross. Therefore **God** highly exalted Him.

When we go back to the Old Testament prophecies we see that a great theme concerning the coming Messiah, Christ, was his sufferings and the glory that would follow, 1 Peter 1:10-11.

> 1 Pet 1:10 Of which salvation the prophets have inquired and searched diligently, who prophesied of the grace that should come unto you: 11 Searching what, or what manner of time the Spirit of Christ which was in them did signify, when it testified beforehand the sufferings of Christ, and the glory that should follow.

And Hebrews says that Christ endured the cross, despising the shame, for the joy that was set before Him (Hebrews 12:2). Jesus understood his own sufferings in the light of his future exaltation and joy.

We remember that the purpose here is not simply to detail the humiliation and exaltation of Christ but to illustrate the principle given in v 5: "Have this attitude in yourselves which was also in Christ Jesus." It is the principle that exaltation only follows humility, the principle found throughout Jesus' teaching and the New Testament:

> Matthew 23:12 Whoever exalts himself shall be humbled, and whoever humbles himself shall be exalted.

> Luke 14:11 For everyone who exalts himself shall be humbled and he who humbles himself shall be exalted.

> 1 Peter 5:6 Humble yourselves therefore under the mighty hand of God that He may exalt you at the proper time.

So that is the main thrust of the passage, that for the Philippians to be lifted up and exalted they must learn humility in the same way as Christ. And this is a principle that we will come back to in Chapter 8 when we consider Christ as our example.

But our concern here is to understand the relationship of Christ's humiliation and exaltation in relation to the subject of the book, the humanity of Christ. And for that we need to pay close attention to what the passage says and actually implies about that. So to that end we will look carefully at the words of the text.

The word *therefore* at the beginning of verse 9 is of great significance. It indicates that this is connected to v 5-8. It is because of his humiliation that God exalted Him. The word *therefore* or *wherefore* has a meaning of being the ground for which the thing that is indicated is done or takes place. The self-emptying of God the Son, his becoming a slave to God's purpose as a man, and accomplishing redemption - all that is the ground for which he is exalted. There is no mention of the glory that Christ had before his self-emptying or restoration of that glory to Him. The ground is entirely what happened in v 5-8.

But didn't Jesus pray for his former glory to be restored (John 17:5)? Yes, He did. And wasn't that to be fulfilled? Yes, it was. But we must not speculate and read that into what is being said here.

And we need to see the source of Jesus' exaltation that is stated **here**. It was **God**: "Therefore also God highly exalted Him . . . ." Jesus' exaltation was not something that He took up for Himself by virtue of being God the Son. It was something that came from God the Father to Jesus as the God-Man. There is a contrast between God and the Son in these words. We have seen that this is the common way that Scripture speaks of God and Christ. God the Father is said to be his God, the God of Christ Jesus.

The word *highly exalted* is a compound in the original language. It includes the preposition *huper* which we find in English in the prefix **hyper** in words like, hypersensitive, hypersonic, and hypertension, with the same idea of being a high degree of something. God "hyperexalted" Christ, lifting Him up.

The exaltation of Christ, however, raises a theological question that is important to our subject. How could Jesus be exalted? He is already God, so how can one who is God be lifted up? We have Jesus' prayer of John 17, "Restore to Me the glory that I had with You before the world began."

That shows without question that He gave up the glory that God would give back to Him. And we see the explanation for what God the Son gave up right here in the preceding verses. But the problem is that here the exaltation of Christ is not declared to be something restored, but something done by God, meaning God the Father. Glory and exaltation are not the same. Exaltation indicates something more.

Consider the glory of God the Son before the incarnation. Was He King of kings? Was He Mediator between God and men? No. To be King of kings, as described in Scripture, He had to come to earth as a man and be crowned and exalted on earth above kings. To be Mediator interceding for those who put their trust in Him, He had to first be a substitutionary sacrifice for them. But Scripture says that Christ was exalted to the right hand of God to be King of kings and be a Mediator.

So something was new in Christ's exaltation that He did not have before. But it was not a new ontological being for God the Son. It was only a new nature, the human nature of Christ that He took on in the incarnation, with new attributes that relate to him in his humanity. This needs to be made clear. We must go into a little detail about what pertains to humanity, being human. Some attributes of human nature are analogous to attributes of deity. These are commonly called the communicable attributes of God. These human attributes that are analogous to divine attributes are what makes a human being in the image of God. Human beings never had and never will have the communicable attributes of God. But they can have attributes analogous to the divine communicable attributes. Of course, by sin those analogous attributes in man were corrupted. And the study of the doctrine of man in the study of Systematic Theology goes into that. It is beyond the scope of the book to review that.

But yes, Jesus **was** exalted by God by virtue of what He accomplished through becoming the God-Man. But we need to stop and think what it was that He did. It was by what He accepted and did through the self-emptying kenosis and acting only with human abilities that there was a reason for his exaltation, and nothing from divine abilities. In his person, ontologically, He was the God-Man. But in terms of what He actually **did,** which was rewarded in his exaltation, it was his human actions alone. And that is exactly what the preceding words in Phil 2 indicate. So the exaltation **requires** that Jesus acted **only** as man.

This is where Jesus' exaltation meets the subject of the book. It was only what He did in his role as man alone that He was exalted.

We have already mentioned Him becoming King of kings and Mediator. Let's detail again more completely the elements of Jesus' exaltation.

In what did this hyperexaltation consist? One element given here is being given a name above every name (v 9). But there are other elements. In Acts 2:32 Peter was preaching: "This Jesus God raised up again." Verse 33, "Therefore having been exalted to the right hand of God." The exaltation of Christ is asserted to have taken place by God raising Jesus from the dead. So being raised from the dead is an element of Jesus' exaltation.

Peter and the Apostles are preaching again: "The God of our fathers raised up Jesus, whom you slew and hanged on a tree. 31, He is the one whom God exalted to His right hand as a prince and a Savior to grant repentance to Israel and forgiveness of sins." They add exaltation as a prince and a savior.

And here something else is added, forgiveness of sin. He intercedes as the one whom God has ordained to forgive sins. Heb 4:14 "He became a high priest who has passed through the heavens." Being high priest indicates intercession.

But passing *through the heavens* indicates something else to become an intercessor, ascending up to the throne of God. It refers to Christ's ascension. The description is expanded in Paul's letter to the Ephesians:

> Eph 1:19 And what is the exceeding greatness of his power to usward who believe, according to the working of his mighty power, 20 Which he wrought in Christ, when he raised him from the dead, and set him at his own right hand in the heavenly places, 21 Far above all principality, and power, and might, and

> dominion, and every name that is named, not only in this world, but also in that which is to come: 22 And hath put all things under his feet, and gave him to be the head over all things to the church,

Being seated at the right hand can be described as a kind of inauguration to kingship, coronation. Coronation precedes actual rule on the earth, which we know in Scripture comes later at Christ's Second Coming to rule over the present earth, which is designated this age (translated *world*) in the Ephesians passage above.

> Romans 14:9 For this end Christ died and lived again that He might be Lord of the dead and the living.

> 1 Cor 15:24 Then comes the end, when He delivers up the Kingdom to the God and Father, when He has abolished all rule and all authority and power. For He must reign until He had put all His enemies under His feet.

John 5 says that God commits all judgment to the Son. God is the source of Christ's exaltation.

And God has committed to Him to be sovereign over everything. That is a role God has given to Him, not something He took up for Himself by right as God the Son restored to his original glory and position.

This again emphasizes that He continues as a man in his exaltation. He is the God-Man yes, with both divine and human nature. He is God the Son yes, as the God-Man ontologically. But to this God-Man is given unique privileges to act as a man, rather than God, until it is turned over to God the Father, as head representing the whole Trinity. This is clear from the fact that it is God in distinction from Him that gives Him the role and the fact that He turns over to God everything at the end.

So we have various elements in Christ's exaltation: resurrection, ascension, coronation at the right hand of God as a Prince, intercession, and then actual rule. And all of these relate to his human role.

Now here Phil 2:9 says that Christ's exaltation includes being given a name above every name. We need to consider the significance of this. We read it was bestowed as a gift. The word here is *echaristo*, with the word *charis*, translated *grace*, right within the word, indicating that it was a gift. So

Christ's position indicated by his name was not only something that He did not have inherently by right as God the Son, but was not even something that He earned! That is surprising. And it is something that needs to be considered carefully.

We see the other things that came about in Jesus' exaltation were things done by God in distinction from Jesus, the God-Man Himself. And what these things are that came about only through both the incarnation as the Son of God, which made it possible, and also the life of Jesus living strictly as a man that was rewarded. But here the name is bestowed as a gift.

We need to be careful here. It does **not** say that Christ's exaltation was a gift and not earned.

God is the source of Christ's exaltation, but Jesus as a perfect man earned it. Here, however, the name by which everyone will bow is bestowed, given as a gift. This also contrasts with the restoring of preincarnate glory, referred to elsewhere. And this is something that can only relate to the God-Man in his human role as an exalted man, because his divine name is inherent and cannot be bestowed as a gift.

Now what is the name which is above every name. It cannot be **Lord.** That is not a name, but a title. But a name is not a mere way of distinguishing one person from another like we use names in our own culture. Throughout Scripture the name relates to something that is true about the person. It is true that Jesus **is** Lord, indicating his lordship. But that is not his name. The name is given right here in the text; it is **Jesus**! It is at the name of **Jesus** that all will bow, which the text actually says. That is the name that will be exalted. Now, of course, many people have been called Jesus, being named after the Lord Jesus Christ. But it will be clear who it is at whose name people will bow. There will be no confusion and people bowing to everyone who happened to be named Jesus by their parents.

There is no need to speculate that Jesus is to be given a new name. The book of Revelation doesn't say so. There is no other place in Scripture that says so, and it does not actually say so here. It is speculation. The word *of* when it says that at the name *of* Jesus, does not indicate a new name different from the name *Jesus*. And the word *bestowed* doesn't indicate a new name. And as mentioned, the name *Jesus* being used of many other people does not indicate it can't be the name bestowed.

When God the Son came into the world He was given or **bestowed** with the name Jesus, meaning Jehovah Saves. That is the etymology of the name *Jesus*. And that is the greatest thing about Jehovah! And it is above everything else revealed about Him! So that, in **fact,** is the name above every name. It is the name God uses of **Himself** that is bestowed! And a name God uses of Himself **has** to be above every other name! The juxtaposition with the phrase "that at the name of Jesus" with what will be his greatest name indicates an identity.

A suggestion has been made that **Lord** is a new name that will be given to Jesus. But that does not sound like a new name. He is already acknowledged as "Lord." When it says a name above every name, it does not have to mean that the name in and of itself indicates exaltation inherently. That pushes language way too far beyond normal usage. A name can **come** to have a signification different from its etymology.

But notice that *Lord* (Greek *kurios*) is a New Testament equivalent to the Old Testament Yahweh, the name of God, Jehovah. That name is embedded in the name Jesus, which we have pointed out, means Jehovah saves. So in a sense the suggestion that there has to be a new name for Jesus reduces the name that He already has.

Now consider the passage that the Apostle Paul takes his statement from. It is the Old Testament Scripture in Isaiah 45:

> Isa 45:21-23 Declare and set forth your case, indeed let them consult together, who has announced this from of old? Who has long since declared it? Is it not I the Lord? (Yahweh, Jehovah) And there is no other God beside Me, a righteous God and a savior. There is none except Me. 22 Turn to Me, and be saved, all the ends of the earth; For I am God and there is no other. 23 I have sworn by Myself, The word has gone forth from My mouth in righteousness and will not turn back, That to Me every knee

will bow, every tongue will swear allegiance.

We must see what Isa 45:22 is actually saying. It is not saying of this only in the future. It is something announced from old that God is the Lord – Jehovah. And this is a call to the ends of the earth from of old, not something only for the future. So the meaning in the New Testament is not that a new name will be given to Jesus, but that in the future people will recognize Jesus and bow at that name, the one who is both God and man. Back in Isa 45:22 it is God from of old who calls to the ends of the earth to turn and be saved. Jehovah, who has always done that, will be recognized to be Jesus, the God-Man.

The context of Isa 45:22 declares specifically what Jehovah God has called out to all the earth from of old. The broader context of Isa 45 is the same as in the New Testament, referring to the future vindication of what God has always called out, that He is Savior, indicated by the name Jesus. And **that** is the reason that it is at the name Jesus, that people will bow in the future.

To make it refer to Jesus' sovereignty misses the point. It is because of Jesus accomplishing perfect righteousness and salvation as a man in the place of sinners that He was exalted and people will bow. The recognition of his sovereignty is for that reason and that alone. Jesus' exalted position and absolute lordship are the consequence of being the perfect man who is Savior, Jesus. Moreover Christians do **not** set aside the name Jesus. That is a fact. They confess that in the name Jesus He must be lord. His lordship is affirmed, but the name does not change.

Jesus is not named Lord, but Jesus is recognized as Lord over and over in the New Testament, over 700 times. That is not his "new"" name. Lordship is attributed to Him, and it is attributed on the grounds of his name, Jesus, Savior.

Conclusion

Christ's exaltation and his incarnation and the kenosis are inextricably linked. Everyone and everything in the universe is now subject to Him. Jesus though hyper-exalted is still in the form of a man, still bears the marks of his first advent, and will continue in that form for ever.

> Acts 19:11 And after He had said these things, He was lifted up while they were looking on, and a cloud received Him out of their sight. 10 And as they were gazing intently into the sky while He was departing, behold, two men in white clothing stood beside them; 11 and they said "men of Galilee, why do you stand looking into the sky? This Jesus, who has been taken up from you into heaven, will come in just the same way as you have watched Him Go into heaven."

Going into heaven didn't change the fact that He was a man who would come to earth again, and we know from Scripture it would be to sit on the throne of David as king of the nation Israel, but in addition to rule the whole world.

> Phil 3:20-21 For our citizenship is in heaven, from which also we eagerly wait for a Savior, the Lord Jesus Christ; who will transform the body of our humble state into conformity with the body of His glory, by the exertion of the power that He has even to subject all things to Himself.

> John 20:19-20 Then, the same day at evening, being the first day of the week, when the doors were shut where the disciples were assembled, for fear of the Jews, Jesus came and stood in the midst, and said to them, peace be with you. 20 When He had said this He showed them His hands and His side. Then the disciples were glad when they saw the Lord.

Jesus' body looked the same but had the ability to appear and disappear. Then Jesus appeared to two disciples on the road to Emmaus and went in to eat with them:

> Luke 24:31 Then their eyes were opened and they knew Him; and He vanished from their sight.

These are just a few examples of his new glorified body. We do not want to read into these examples too much and enter into speculation, but we can see a definite change in his role as a person, and Scripture says that at his appearing we will be like Him, a glorified man.

> 1 John 3:2 Beloved, now we are children of God; and it has not

yet been revealed what we shall be, but we know that when He is revealed, we shall be like Him, for we shall see Him as He is.

It is significant, as noted before, to remember that while Jesus' humiliation (kenosis) has ended and the access to and exercise of divine prerogatives and glory are restored to Him, the incarnation itself has not ended. The Son of God in becoming a man entered a new permanent state. That means, and we stress emphatically, Christ Jesus is still one hundred percent man, and one hundred percent God, and all the parameters recorded in the Scripture as spelled out by Chalcedon and historic Christianity remain true.

The God-Man, who is both divine and glorified in his humanity, having two natures in one person, is now and has for the last two millennia, been given access to his former glories. What is very relevant to our discussion of Christ's humanity is that He is even now also exercising his glorified human nature and the corresponding attributes.

Obviously when we view Christ or picture Him in our mind's eye we are seeing a single person, the glorified man, son of Mary, son of David, yes. But we know and are taught by Scripture He is one Christ including two natures, one visible and one nature invisible which possesses the entire nature of God including all of God's glories deriving from the one divine essence.

6.

CHRIST AS PROPHET

We have seen the biblical teaching that Jesus lived his life during his state of humiliation until his resurrection was by faith and not by sight. And we have seen how it teaches that He acted in his miracles by the power of the Holy Spirit. The importance of Chapter 3 concerning Jesus' humanity is absolutely germane to our understanding of his person and work. It helps us to appreciate Christ's office as prophet which is also crucial to realize and to help comprehend his humanity. Application of it answers a number of reasonable questions that can be raised that otherwise could not be answered. Chapter 3 regarding the biblical doctrine of Christ's humanity lays the proper foundation for his office of prophet. There were and are specific qualifications which a prophet must meet. There are also very important guidelines a prophet must follow during his ministry under the penalty of death (Deut 18:20-22). For Jesus to be a prophet, meeting the qualifications of a prophet, He could not be an exception to this.

The fact that Jesus has the office of prophet applies also to his earthly ministry as a man. This is treated more fully and so separately here from the other teachings about how Jesus lived in the state of his humiliation because of the prominence and ramifications given to it in Scripture, even if it seems repetitive. The designation in Scripture of Jesus as a Prophet is as outstanding as Him being Priest and Sacrifice, and being the Messianic King of Israel and the world.

Scripture makes the fact of his being the fulfillment of Moses' prophesy in Deut 18:15 very clear by the statement of Peter in Acts 3:22:

> "Moses said , 'The LORD God shall raise up for you a prophet like me from among your brethren; to Him you shall gtive heed in everything He says to you."

Peter and John had just healed a lame man and then launched into a long sermon to his countrymen all about Jesus being the Christ and includes also that He was that prophet who was to come. This leaves no room for doubt that Jesus was Israel's prophesied Prophet who was to come. Luke quotes the Apostle Peter who quotes the Prophet Moses, saying "The Lord God shall raise up for you a prophet like me from your brethren; to Him you shall give heed in everything He says to you". And in addition, Steven also attests to this same fact in Acts 7:37.

Luke 24:27 should be understood to include this: "And beginning with Moses and with all the prophets, He explained to them all the things concerning Himself in all the Scriptures." We are not told what Jesus said to them, but we can be sure that being the prophet who was to come from among their countrymen would be one of the "all things" concerning Himself that He would have explained.

But did Jesus meet the qualifications for being a human prophet of God? The answer is, Yes he did! First we can see in Scripture what the qualifications were, and then we can see how Jesus met them:

We look first at Deut 18:20 "But the prophet who shall speak a word presumptuously in My name which I have not commanded him to speak, or which he shall speak in the name of other gods, that prophet shall die."

What this says is that a prophet shall not speak anything from within himself, or from his own experience, or from his own wisdom, or any other source other than hearing it directly from the one true God. What this means is that Jesus, since He was a man, could never even once speak from his own authority, but that whatever He spoke, He received from God his Father through the Holy Spirit.

That Jesus met this prerequisite is stated in the Gospel of John:

John 12:49-50 For I did not speak on my own initiative, but the Father Himself who sent Me has given Me commandment what to say, and what to speak. 50. And I know that His commandment is eternal life; therefore the thing I speak, I speak just as the Father has told Me.

Here Jesus is telling us directly that He did not speak from his own initiative. But because Jesus is both God and Man having divine and human natures but being one person, He did not speak from either human or divine initiative either, for if He did He would be acting as one of two persons, rather than one person. And we have already seen that in his person Christ is one person with two natures, not two persons. He rather spoke from his person, rather than speaking from a nature. A nature does not exercise initiative but provides for the ability of a person to exercise initiative. It is the person who acts. It sounds technical but it is important to preserve the true Christology that was explained in Chapter 2.

> John 17:8 for the words which Thou gavest Me I have given to them; and they have received them, and truly understood that I came forth from Thee, and they believed that Thou didst send Me.

Here Jesus is attributing what He said to words that were given to Him. They were not his words. So again Jesus met the requirement of not speaking from Himself but receiving the words he was to speak from God, as is required of a prophet of God.

> John 3:34 For He whom God has sent speaks the words of God; for He gives the Spirit without measure.

Jesus is referring to Himself in referring to "He whom God has sent." Again it means that He distinguishes Himself from God, God the Father. And the way He knows God's words is indicated as being by "the Spirit without measure."

> John 7:16 My teaching is not mine but His who sent Me.

Jesus again denies that what He teaches comes from Himself personally. This is consistent with the requirement that a prophet must not speak his own thoughts.

> John 8:26 The things I heard from Him, these things I speak to the world.

Over and over, Jesus expresses the same thought in different ways.

> John 8:28 I do nothing on My own initiative, but I speak these things as the Father taught Me.

What we saw in John 12:49 was stated by Jesus earlier.

> John 8:40 But you seek to kill Me, a man who has told You the truth, which I heard from God; this Abraham did not do.

The truth, the words that Jesus gave, He heard from God, distinguishing them from his own words.

> John 14:10 Do you not believe that I am in the Father, And the Father is in Me? The words that I say to you I do not speak on My own initiative, but the Father abiding in Me does His works.

Here is a yet another time in which Jesus says the same thing. The literal rendering for "My own initiative" in John 8:28, 12:49, and 14:10 is "not from myself" or "not out of myself."

Over and over we see Scripture declaring the very thing that is given as a qualification for being a prophet that he would **not** be speaking from his own knowledge, or by something other than receiving the words from God, God the Father. And Jesus emphasizes this, that He Himself **received** his words from God and were **not** from Himself. It is hard to see how it could be clearer than that He was declaring that as man, while also being very God, the Son of God, that He was not using his divine abilities.

Much is said comparing Jesus to the other prophets, but the significance of Jesus Himself being a prophet seems to get overlooked. Yet this is a very significant part of who the Messiah/Christ is. When John the Baptist was asked about being Messiah, we see how he answered:

> John 1:19 The Jews sent to him priests and Levites from Jerusalem to ask him, "Who are you?" 20 And he confessed, and did not deny, and he confessed, "I am not the Christ." 21 And they asked him, "what then? Are you Elijah?" And he said, "I am not." "Are you the Prophet?" And he answered, "No."

John's answer is very interesting since he also was in fact a prophet of the one true God. He was a prophet who was to come and herald the coming of the one true prophet who was to be like Moses.

This was recognized by others too, on the basis of the miracle of the feeding of the five thousand:

> John 6:14 "When therefore the people saw the sign which He had

performed, they said, 'This is of a truth the Prophet who is to come into the world'."

This was a reference to the great prophet following Moses.

But let's compare Jesus with the Apostle Peter. He along with John performed miracles and spoke for God, acting as a prophet in the proper sense of the term. We see this in Acts 3:1-16. Peter and John came upon a man lame from his mother's womb, and they healed him so that all could see the miracle. The crowd was full of amazement, and Peter said (v 12) : "Men of Israel, why do you marvel at this, or why do you gaze at us, as if by our own power or piety we had made him walk?" Peter goes on to say it was the God of Abraham, Isaac, and Jacob who glorified his servant Jesus, and He goes further, it was on the basis of faith in his name that the man was made whole. The idea of any man doing a miracle like this is preposterous, no matter what slight of hand or conniving he used. Nevertheless it did appear to the crowd as though Peter and John did have the power to perform this miracle. Interrupting the natural order of things is a glory that belongs to God alone that He says He will not share with another. God does in fact perform miracles when his plan calls for it. And this is exactly what Jesus continually taught his disciples. Peter was a prophet in every sense of the word and God performed many miracles through him. Every miracle Peter performed was to confirm him as a messenger with a word from God. The miracles authenticated that the message was from the only one who had this power, God Himself.

It is biblically sound to compare Moses to Jesus since the Holy Spirit makes this comparison between the two men in Heb 3:1-3 "Therefore, holy brethren, partakers of a heavenly calling, consider Jesus, the Apostle and High Priest of our confession. 2 He was faithful to Him who appointed Him, as Moses was in all his house. 3 For He has been counted worthy of more glory than Moses, by just so much as the builder of the house has more honor as the house."

In Exod 4:1-17 God enlists Moses as a prophet who will represent Him in freeing his elect Israel from their 400 year bondage to Egypt. In Exod 3:20 God says to Moses, "So I will stretch out My hand, and strike Egypt with all My miracles which I shall do in the midst of it; and after that he will let you go." Then Moses answered and said (Exod 4:1), "What if they will not believe me, or listen to what I say? For they may say, 'the Lord has not appeared to you.'" Then as the account goes God turns Moses' staff into a serpent and back again to a staff, followed by Moses' hand being stricken with leprosy and healed just as quickly. Later in Num 20:1-13 Moses sinned by striking the rock to bring forth water instead of speaking to the rock as God instructed him to do. This made the power look like it was coming from Moses instead of from God and Moses' disobedience kindled God's jealousy and Moses was punished severely. The point is that Scripture teaches that if God uses men to perform a miracle they should not give the impression that the power was their own or take credit in any way for it. All prophets when performing a miracle are to perform them in the same way, by faith, calling on the power of God. Then God actually performs the miracle with his own intrinsic power through the circumstantial agency of his prophets. We observe that Jesus as the prophet of God always made sure to the watching world that the power was not coming from Him personally but from God.

The following illustrates this very strikingly:

In the account of Jesus raising Lazarus from the dead, Martha says (John 11:22), "Even now I know that whatever you ask of God, God will give you." And Jesus responded, "Father, I thank Thee that though heardest Me. And I knew that thou hearest Me always; but because of the people standing around I said it, that they may believe that Thou didst send Me (v 41-42)."

The tendency is to read into this miracle that Jesus because of the fact that Scripture teaches that the universe was created by Him, so that He is the giver of life, the source of life and that there was nothing made that He did not make, so that all things subsist by the word of his power, therefore Jesus as God by his own divine power raised Lazarus. But that does not comport with what Jesus actually said and did. He was consistent with living life as a man and acting as a prophet like the man Moses. This left Him one option, which was to call on God like all men must do. Notice that

Jesus did not say to the Father "that they may believe that I am God the Son," but "that Thou didst send Me." That was the first and important issue. That He was therefore also God in the flesh would follow.

Jesus often spoke things no ordinary man could know, even things that were not previously revealed in the Old Testament. We remember the people exclaiming "never a man spoke like this man". This is taken to mean that He spoke from his divine knowledge that He had by being omniscient. However, Moses also spoke things no man could possibly know. For instance Moses revealed to us the creation of the earth, and the formation of the first man out of the earth's dirt, the fall of mankind into sin, the flood, and so forth. We have just seen that Jesus says repeatedly his words were not his own but were those of his Father who sent Him. So we **must** conclude that the things that no ordinary man could know were delivered to Him by divine revelation like those things delivered to other prophets, including Moses by divine revelation. Moreover, if Jesus had the knowledge of these things, He would not have needed to ask the Father for the words as He said he did when He was about to raise Lazarus. This is proof that He was speaking by divine revelation just as a prophet would.

There were many times where the Old Testament lacked the details of a prophesied event but then these were elucidated by Jesus in fulfilling the particular event. These are cases of greater revelation through Jesus of the meaning of an earlier prophesy. An example is Jesus' entry into Jerusalem in the last week of his life. He was fully aware of Zech 9:9 "Behold your king is coming to you; He is just and endowed with salvation, humble and mounted on a donkey, even a colt, the foal of a donkey." But knowing exactly who had the donkey and exactly where it was and so forth are details not prophesied in the Old Testament, yet necessary for Jesus to know in order to facilitate the event. Here it is possible He could be acting as the Great Prophet.

The building of the church began upon the foundation being laid by the apostles and prophets. We read in Eph 2:20 "Having been built upon the foundation of the apostles and prophets, Christ Jesus Himself being the corner stone." Here

110

Christ as the corner stone is put side by side with prophets. He as the Great Prophet Himself was the corner stone. Again He is identified as a prophet.

There is no doubt that Jesus was the prophet of Deut 18:15, but there is a failure to consistently follow through with the implications of this truth. This fulfilled prophesy of Jesus being the prophet of Deut 18, should give us a clearer picture of the man Jesus the Christ both in his person and in explaining his works.

Now we must not confuse things. In saying Jesus was a human prophet like Moses there is absolutely **no** suggestion that Jesus was just another prophet in the long line of prophets. He was by his credentials the most unique prophet of all. Jesus using only the powers available to other men like Moses and Elijah elevated the office of prophet to a new level. And saying this certainly does not suggest that He was a mere man.

While Scripture shows conclusively that the Son of God was that prophet who was to come, we ask the question why a prophet? If God sent his Son as the exact representation of Himself, who is perfect with every divine quality belonging to God, why was there any need for Him to be a prophet like Moses? Was it not enough God sending his own Son as Israel's Messiah to reconcile the world to Himself? Isaiah prophesied the Messiah would be a man child, God with us. In this there was a prophecy that the Messiah be both God and man. We know that part of the truth, that He would need to be a real man to accomplish the human part of propitiation and salvation, and He would need to be really God for the value of his propitiation and sacrifice to avail for many to be saved. Yet it was also prophesied that He would perform the many functions of a great prophet, including miracles. So why?

We saw before, it was to identify Him as coming from God, and therefore clearly identifying Him along with other fulfillments of Scripture as the one who would be "God with us." So there is no question that his miracles identified Him as God indeed, but not directly.

The word *Messiah/Christ* simply means an anointed one,

but the future Messiah would be the coming worldwide ruler and deliverer of his people. In the New Testament the word *anointed* translated into Greek and then English becomes *Christ*. So accepting Jesus as the Christ, means accepting Him as the coming worldwide ruler and deliverer. But we must understand that He would not just deliver people externally, but also from their sins – redeem them from the pending wrath of God. The Messiah/Christ was to hold all three offices of Prophet, Priest and King, with their respective functions, and all three were absolutely necessary to the eternal plan to redeem man and conform him to the image of his Son.

When God says something "has" to be, we must take him at his word. And when He says Jesus was a prophet, we must believe Him and let The New Testament narratives portray him as prophet acting as a prophet. The fact that Jesus was a prophet is not only true but it was absolutely necessary. And when He said the prophet would be selected from among his country men and be like Moses, we should accept it at face value and trust Him.

Prayer is an indication of Jesus as a man before God. The alternative that He needed to spend that time as God the Son to commune with God the Father doesn't make sense, knowing what we do about the Trinity. Only if it was Jesus as man, does this make sense. Prayer is primarily asking God to do what He has revealed in Scripture that He will do, and only secondarily what we would like. In the case of Jesus, as a prophet, He would receive that knowledge by special revelation in addition to Scripture that already existed. But He would need to know the specifics of what He should do by that special revelation. And Scripture shows that He waited upon his Father for that knowledge, because He spent all night in prayer. In places where what He prayed is reported there is no sign that it was purely inter-Trinitarian.

And there is one other most important point that needs to be brought out. In saying that Jesus could not speak from Himself as a prophet but rely entirely and only on what was revealed to Him, we need to take into account the true Christology of Chapter 2. It was not Jesus in his human nature that was limited to receiving and speaking only what was revealed to Him. It was Jesus as a person, the divine and human natures conjoined in perfect harmony that was limited in this way. To say that it was Jesus **only** in his human nature that was limited and that He could still use his divine nature would be to reintroduce the Nestorian error. The two natures would be two separate persons acting in one human body. No, it was Jesus Himself as a person, both divine and human, that was limited to not speaking from Himself. That is the requirement of a prophet of God.

So now we see something that was not clear in the preceding chapters. Not only is what Jesus did entirely explainable in terms of the biblical doctrine of Christ's human life, but it is necessary. To be a true prophet of God it was a requirement that He **not** use his divine power of omniscience. Up to this point there was only a presumption that Jesus did not use any of his divine powers during his state of humiliation on earth. Now we see that it is more than a presumption that He did not do so, but a requirement for Him not to use his divine power of omniscience to be a true prophet of God.

7.

IMPLICATIONS OF THE DOCTRINES
OF THE ATONEMENT AND JUSTIFICATION
FOR CHRIST'S HUMANITY

In Chapters 1 and 2 we affirmed the biblical truths concerning the one true God, the Trinity, and the incarnation of God the Son as the God-Man, Christ, both fully God and fully man. Here in this Chapter we affirm the truths of God's plan of salvation for men, and see how the doctrines of the atonement and justification by grace alone through faith alone in Christ alone on the grounds of the sacrifice of Christ alone become significant for Christ's humanity.

God's Plan of Salvation

What is a person's greatest spiritual need? It is to be saved from sin and its consequences. In brief, the consequence of sin is that God rejects people because of it and condemns them to an eternal existence in hell. That is the stark reality that people either want to put out of their thoughts or will try to ridicule.

So what does a person have to do for God to accept him? According to the Bible it is repent and trust Jesus. A person is saved from sin and its consequences by Jesus Christ. So who was Jesus Christ? It is really very important to be able to answer these questions because it is crucial to one's eternal destiny. Jesus Christ is God's Son and it is by what He did that people can be saved from their sins.

But suppose that a person has answered that a person's greatest spiritual need is God's salvation, that Jesus Christ is the Son of God, and that a person must accept Jesus Christ as his personal Savior for God to accept him. It needs to be asked what it **means** for one to accept Christ as his personal Savior. Perfunctory answers are all too common, and do not show that there is no deficiency in understanding. A person may be sincere but not have understood the requirements of true repentance and faith. People just do not consider the possibility of self-deception.

But basically the good news is that God accepts people who come to Him in Christ, without considering anything that they have done or failed to do. That is amazing. But just **how** is that possible?

What people need to know are the truths that God is the eternal, holy Creator and Ruler; that man is rebellious and depraved, though in the image of God; that Christ as God's Son is the Redeemer of those who become truly converted, who are born of God and who turn in repentance and faith to Christ; and that Christ will come to right all things, and that He will judge sinful men who reject his gospel; and finally that one must himself **personally** come to Christ for God to accept him and give him eternal salvation.

1. The eternal, sovereign Creator and Ruler.

The Bible teaches that God is love, but it also teaches that the wrath of God now abides on those who do not believe in Christ (John 3:36). Scripture nowhere says that God loves the sinner but hates his sin. It does say that God is angry with the sinner continually. People raise such questions as, "How can there be a good God that allows physical evil?" It shows a basic misunderstanding of the nature of God. Sin **does** exist and suffering does **also**. Therefore, if there is a God, He is not the "good god" that men think. The question is how God, who is eternal, holy, and good, could allow suffering to exist in the world. Of course, suffering is not always evil. For example, pain is necessary for a person to avoid harm, like a child who gets burned slightly. He learns to avoid touching a hot stove and getting burned seriously. The Bible teaches that after man first sinned, God cursed the earth for man's sake (Gen 3:17-19). But in addition, hardship and natural disasters are a warning that God is not what people often picture Him to be, a god who will not let men suffer, such as suffering eternally for their sins. We have to lay to rest the idea that God can be anything else than what He reveals Himself to be.

He reveals in the Bible that He is sovereign: He has the right to create, to rule, and to set standards according to his own will. If there is a God He is sovereign, or He wouldn't really be God. According to the Bible, God says, "I am God, and there is none like me, declaring the end from the beginning, and from the ancient times the things that are not yet done, saying, My counsel shall stand, and I will do all my pleasure" (Isa 46:9-10). He created the world, and He has power over his own creation. God is a God who can do as He pleases. That is why He also says, "I form the light, and create darkness: I make peace, and create evil: I the LORD do all these things" (Isa 45:7), and "Woe unto him that striveth with his Maker!" (Isa 45:9).

People don't like this picture of God. They want to be free to do what they think is right, and they don't want anyone telling them what they can or can't do, even the God who made them.

2. God's Holiness and Man's Sin and Depravity.

The Bible also teaches that God created man in his own image (Gen 1:27), with true knowledge (Col 3:10) and righteousness (Eph 4:24). Because he was created in God's image, man is capable of receiving revelation from Him, and this is shown in the book of Romans: "Because that which may be known of God is manifest in them; for God hath shewed it unto them" (Rom 1:19). In other words, built into themselves is something that shows men what God is like. And it says, "For the invisible things from the creation of the world are clearly seen, being understood by the things that are made, even his eternal power and Godhead" (Rom 1:20). So even the creation shows that God is sovereign. But men have sinned, and so it is written, "When they knew God, they glorified him not as God, neither were thankful; but became vain in their imaginations, and their foolish heart was darkened" (Rom 1:21). They "changed the truth of God into a lie, and worshiped and served the creature rather than the Creator" (Rom 1:25). People must worship something, and if they don't worship God, they will worship idols, nature, religion, wealth, or they will worship the product of their own minds, or even other men. They have insulted and rejected the infinite and holy God. How does God respond to that? What God actually did was to give people up to their own corrupt natures. Look at the

116

description here in Romans chapter 1 (Rom 1:28-32). Deep within them men know that they have sinned against God and that what they do is against his just standard, his law. That is what sin is - lawlessness (I John 3:4), and Jesus summarized God's law this way, "Thou shalt love the Lord thy God with all thy heart, and with all thy soul, and with all thy mind." And, "Thou shalt love thy neighbor as thyself" (Matt 22:3 7, 39). In other words, sin consists of what we think and feel, as well as what we do; it consists of what we have neglected, as well as what we have done wrong. And God holds every bit of this against us. That is especially true for those who put the thought of God entirely out of their minds and pretend He does not even exist.

Not only is it true that sins are against a God who is infinite. Sin requires an infinite punishment! This is why finite people can never make up for their sins. And no one can make up for it with good deeds, because the Bible also says "But we are as an unclean thing, and all our righteousnesses – our good deeds - are as filthy rags" (Isa 64:6). But then, too, our finite good deeds could never make up for the infinite wrong against the infinite God. And God is holy. There is no way out for Himself. God by his very nature has no choice but must punish sin. "But the LORD of hosts shall be exalted in judgment, and God that is holy shall be sanctified in righteousness" (Isa 5:16). God is "of purer eyes than to behold evil, and can'st not look on iniquity (Hab 1:13).

If all this is so, how in the world is it possible for God to ever accept anyone who has sinned? In the first place, God is merciful in postponing his judgment on us. He is good to both just and unjust people, letting them both enjoy sun, rain, and food, and good things (Matt 5:45; Acts 14:17) while they last. And if one person harms another, the one who is harmed does not suffer more than he deserves in God's sight. And a holy and just God will not let them go free. But there is another reason why God postpones his judgment. God is merciful, so that some will have the opportunity to be saved from judgment by Christ and what He has done.

3. God's Provision of Redemption in Christ.

Jesus Himself said, I am the way, the truth, and the life: no man cometh unto the Father – God - but by me" (John 14:6). It seems completely unreasonable for anyone to say that he is the one way men can come to God, doesn't it? So how could Jesus have the right to say that? First, he would have to have kept God's law perfectly and be sinless. And the Scripture says that he "was in all points tempted like as we are, yet without sin" (Heb 4:15). Christ was predicted long before to be the sinless, human substitute to pay the penalty for sin. In that way he could be the one way men can come to God. God's Word says that God "shall see the travail of his soul, and shall be satisfied: by knowledge of him shall *his* righteous servant justify many; for he shall bear their iniquities" (Isa 53:11). That's what Christ's death on the Cross means. Christ suffered for their sins, in the place of sinful men. As sinful man could not pay the penalty for another's sin; he must pay for his own sin. Jesus could only pay the penalty for another's sin, by being sinless.

But the suffering and death of one finite man could never pay the penalty for the sins of many people against an infinite God. Even a sinless, perfect man, because he is finite, could only pay the penalty for one other person. To satisfy God's justice, the payment for many people could only be sufficient if Jesus Christ Himself were more than finite - if He were Himself God. And that is what Scripture says: "In him dwelleth all the fulness of the Godhead bodily" (Col 2:9). That is the meaning of Jesus' birth. What happened is called the incarnation. Jesus was a perfect, sinless man, but also infinite God; and because God has power over his creation, He could send his eternal Son into the world in this way: "For God so loved the world, that he gave his only begotten Son, his eternal Son, that whosoever believeth in him should not perish, but have everlasting life. For God sent not his Son into the world to condemn the world; but that the world through him might be saved" (John 3:16-17). "But when the fulness of the time was come, God sent forth his Son, made of a woman, made under the law (Gal 4:4).

4. God's requirements.

But unless the Spirit of God has been working in a person's

heart and he is born again and have a spiritual birth —he cannot enter into God's kingdom or be accepted by God. It says, "Except a man be born of water and the Spirit, he cannot enter into the kingdom of God" (John 3:5), and "But as many as received him, to them gave he the right to become the children of God - accepted by God - even to them that believe on his name: which were born, not of blood, nor of the will of the flesh, nor of the will of man, but of God" (John 1:12-13). So there must be a change in one's heart, so that he becomes a new creation in Christ: new motives, new desires, and new ways of thinking. And that is not the kind of change a person by himself can make within himself. But there is something that God commands a person to do: repent and trust Christ (Acts 20:21). But repentance is not just being sorry for ones sins: "Godly sorrow worketh repentance to salvation not to be repented of: but the sorrow of the world worketh death" (2 Cor 7:10). It is turning away from one's sins and the flesh, and turning away from the world and all that it stands for (John 17:16; 15:19). It means giving up the past life that we have been living. And that is why God has to do the work within, because only He can change our hearts to make us willing to do that much, and only He can give the power to carry it out. If real repentance is to take place, the person who repents must depend entirely on God. The other thing that goes along with that is faith. God says that men are to trust, believe in, or have faith in Christ. Jesus said, "He that believeth on me hath everlasting life" (John 6:47). To believe **on** Him means to believe in Him as He really is. He is God's Son, and that means that He has the right to rule over us and direct our lives. We must commit ourselves to Him and receive Him as Lord and Savior. Then He promises that God will accept us and make us his children. That means we must put our eternal destiny in the hands of Jesus Christ and follow Him. And it is not just that God gives people an opportunity; He commands people to be saved from their sin and the judgment due to them for it. He accepts every one who repents —and turns from his own way and his sin to trust Christ.

5. The Consummation and Judgment.

The Bible says that Christ not only died on the Cross for sin, but he arose from the dead and appeared to the early disciples (1 Cor 15). "God also hath highly exalted him, and given him a name which is above every name: That at the name of Jesus every knee should bow . . . and every tongue should confess that Jesus Christ is Lord, to the glory of God the Father" (Phil 2:8-11). This is why Jesus could say that those who condemned Him to death would see Him again "sitting on the right hand of power, and coming in the clouds of heaven" (Mark 14:62). When He comes again He will rule on the earth and make everything right. God says, "Yea, all kings shall fall before him; all nations shall serve him. For he shall deliver the needy . . . " (Psalm 72:11-12), and, "In his day shall the righteous flourish; and abundance of peace so long as the moon endureth. He shall have dominion also from sea to sea, and from the river unto the ends of the earth. They that dwell in the wilderness shall bow before him; and his enemies shall lick the dust" (Psalm 72:7-9). "For he must reign till he hath put all enemies under his feet" (1 Cor 15:25), and ". . . he shall rule them with a rod of iron" (Rev 19:15). And not only that, all those who are in Christ will be caught up to be with Christ when He comes: the dead in Christ shall be raised first and then the others in Christ (1 Thes 4:16-17). And God has promised that they shall reign with Christ on the earth (Rev 5:10) and judge the world with him (1 Cor 6:2). But for those who are not Christ's we read: that "the Lord Jesus shall be revealed from heaven with his mighty angels, in flaming fire taking vengeance on them that know not God and that obey not the gospel of our Lord Jesus Christ" (2 Thes 1:7-8). And Jesus said, "For the Father judgeth no man, but hath committed all judgment unto the Son "; "marvel not at this: for the hour is coming, in the which all that are in the graves shall hear his voice, and shall come forth; they that have done good, unto the resurrection of life; and they that have done evil, unto the resurrection of damnation "(John 5:22). 28-29). Some will go away into everlasting punishment (Matt 24:46). But the everlasting fire that Jesus spoke of was not created for men; it was prepared for the devil and his angels (Matt 24:41).

6. The Gospel Call

In view of the impossibility to do anything but accept God's way to be saved it is clear that one cannot be saved of works, but only by God's grace. (Eph 2:8-9) "But to him that worketh not, but believeth on him that justifieth the ungodly, his faith is counted for righteousness" (Rom 4:5). God counts the person's trust in Christ and what He has done for righteousness. He transfers the righteousness of Christ, his payment of the penalty and his righteous life, over to the person's account. That is how God accepts men who come to Him in Christ without considering anything they have done or failed to do. But there must be a real commitment to Christ. And that must be done by calling upon Christ. "For whosoever shall call upon the name of the Lord shall be saved" (Rom 10:13). A person must himself personally close with Christ. Scripture says it is necessary to call upon the Lord and confess with the mouth to God (Rom 10:8-13).

The above is the message of salvation to lost sinners and embodies the basic truths concerning God's plan of salvation. With that foundation we are in a position to see how the truths concerning Christ's life as a man clarify the biblical teachings concerning Christ's atoning work and the doctrine of justification.

Without the biblical doctrine of Christ's humanity, Christ could not have redeemed men from sin. So the biblical doctrine has implications for the doctrine of Christ's atonement and *vice versa*. By atonement is meant what God has done to actually bring fallen man and Himself together. It includes both what Christ accomplished by his life laid down at the Cross, his expiation, and the action by which God is able to accept an individual repentant believer in Christ, which is justification on the grounds of the imputed righteousness of Christ.

Four Questions

Using the method we have followed before we ask questions and give answers.

1. First Question

Was it necessary for the sacrifice of Christ to provide

penal satisfaction in order to satisfy God's justice? Or instead was it only necessary for it either (1) to function only as a moral influence to induce people to see the seriousness of sin and the great love of God so that they would turn to Him? or (2) only as a manifestation and vindication of God's just government but not truly required by God's attribute of justice.

Scripture teaches without any question that the love of God causes those who believe to love him in return. We read this in just so many words in 1 John 4:19 "We love him, because he first loved us." So God, in order to save us, sent Christ to die to melt our hearts so that we would repent and come to Christ. And "God commendeth his love toward us, in that, while we were yet sinners, Christ died for us" (Rom 5:8). So God's love was indeed a motive. But Scripture teaches that it was not the only motive. God by his very nature had to turn away his wrath due to his holiness and provide satisfaction because of his just nature. So the moral influence view of the atonement falls short of the requirements of God's very nature, and substitutes a false god.

But in the present day there are many who profess to believe the teaching of the Bible who do not accept that the atonement was by way of penal satisfaction of God's inherent justice. This also is a matter of the nature of God Himself. It is beyond the scope of the book to deal with the error that God's own nature did not required Him to pour out his wrath on Christ in order to save men, but rather the false idea that He chose to do so for reasons other than his inherent justice. Many shrink from the moral influence view of blatant modernism yet reject penal satisfaction.

But this other governmental view is of significance because it also makes the incarnation and Christ's perfect life less than necessary. Careful thinkers have argued that it really can be reduced to the moral influence view when pressed to its logical conclusion.

Then there is the so-called ethical view. This is very much like the governmental view by also making God's justice a matter of God's will rather than something required by

God's nature. God can by a mere act of will set aside his justice if his moral nature is satisfied by the Cross of Christ. This is a more subtle attack on the nature of God, and again is beyond the scope of the book to deal with except to mention it.

2. Second Question

Could Christ satisfy God in his sacrifice on the Cross through the ontological fact of being both fully God and fully man, without having lived his life only as a man in a state of humiliation?

The answer is, No. The sacrifice had to be of like kind as the one who commits the sin. It was a man who sinned and violated God, so it had to be a man, who provides satisfaction. But it could not be any man, but a perfect man who must die to accomplish the necessary satisfaction. It is true, the fact of Christ being ontologically fully human and fully God was needed to accomplish in his flesh all of the things necessary for Him to be a perfect sacrifice, or a spotless lamb, or the perfect substitute. But it remained to be seen if Jesus was able to live out a perfectly righteously life. If Jesus had fallen short of keeping the law at every point in his life while attempting to please his Father, his sacrifice would not have been acceptable.

The idea of a perfect substitutionary sacrifice is taught in many ways through the Old Testament, especially through the ceremonial law. The book of Hebrews explains how the sacrificial animal is a pattern or type of One who would come. We are told that those sacrifices, because not of a person, could never take away sin. But why a sacrifice at all, especially a human sacrifice of one who lived a perfect innocent life?

Eze 18:4 "The soul who sins will die." The soul in this case is the soul or life of a person, any and all who have ever sinned. "God's eyes are too pure to approve evil, and Thou canst not look on wickedness with favor" (Hab 1:13). Therefore God pronounces the curse of death on all who violate his law, who sin.

But Ezekiel tells us (Eze18:32) " 'For I have no pleasure in the death of anyone who dies', declares the Lord

123

God.'Therefore, repent and live'." Eze 33:11 "Say to them, 'As I live!' declares the Lord God, 'I take no pleasure in the death of the wicked, but rather that the wicked turn from his way and live'." Since all have sinned, and God takes no pleasure in carrying out the punishment of death, He provided a way to reconcile a sinner to Himself.

The Apostle John begins to clarify for us how it is possible for God to save men from the death curse of God and his wrath. John 3:16 "For God so loved the world, that He gave His only begotten Son, that whoever believes in Him should not perish, but have eternal life." But what does all this mean? It certainly means that a person has to repent to find out what it means, for if one repents he in effect has believed the gospel, and repentance is a fruit of faith in what the gospel says. And what the gospel says is that while a person is spiritually dead because of his sins against God, God loved enough to send someone, another human being like the one who repents and believes, and the One that He sent was perfect and sinless. Without being affected by that love and understanding that God sent One who was willing to take his sins and the punishment that otherwise would be due, and to suffer and die in his place, a person would never believe the gospel in the first place. So it is only a matter of filling in the blanks surrounding this mystery.

God explains it starting with 2 Cor 5:19 "namely, that God was in Christ reconciling the world to Himself, not counting their trespasses against them." Since Christ was willing to become man and emptied Himself of the exercise of divine powers, as we have explained in Chapter 5, He was able to accomplish all that was necessary to propitiate and satisfy the wrath of God the Father who sent Him. But our question is, was this atonement possible for the Son of God without successfully living his whole life in humiliation as a man? Again we refer to Heb 2:17 "Therefore He had to be made like His brethren in all things, that He might become a merciful and faithful high priest in things pertaining to God, to make propitiation for the sins of the people." This *had* to include what He did as well as what He **was** ontologically. It would not be possible for Jesus to just be ontologically God and man to satisfy or propitiate God without accomplishing living under the law of God; otherwise He would be acting as God, not under the law and not as a man under the law, and not like his brethren in **all** things. And that is where Gal 3:20 comes in: "Now a mediator is not for one *party only,* whereas God is *only* one." This speaks of his actions as man, not of his being or ontology. Mediating between two parties is an action or activity. And here it says explicitly God is **one,** meaning that He was not mediating within Himself, God the Son with God the Father. Rather it was a representative of men, a man approaching God as one other than God, specifically a priest.

But in addition, since it was not God who sinned but a man who sinned, it was a man who needed to make amends. Christ then had to live his whole life as a perfect man for that life to satisfy for the whole life of sin and degradation and sinful actions of another. But in addition being ontologically the same as the one for whom He would be the substitute, He also, of course, needed to be God for the sacrifice to have infinite value so that it would satisfy for more than one person. And the violation was perpetrated against a divine person, so the punishment had to be infinite for that reason as well, which is why the sentence of death is a sentence of eternal death.

The question that we have been answering was: Because Jesus was in fact ontologically both God and man, was it necessary for Him to live a human life when He lived in the state of humiliation? Scripture gives another answer; it tells us as a matter of fact that is exactly how He lived his life:

Gal 4:4 But when the fullness of time came, God sent forth His Son, Born of a woman under the law, v 5 in order that He might redeem those who were under the law, that we might receive the adoption as sons.

Luke 2:52 And Jesus kept increasing in wisdom and stature, and in favor with God and man.

Heb 4:15 For we do not have a high priest who can not sympathize with our weaknesses, but one who has been tempted in all things as we are, yet without sin.

Heb 5:8 All though He was a Son, He learned obedience from the things which He suffered." v 9 And having been made perfect, He became to all those who obey Him the source of eternal salvation."

Here we reiterate what we brought up in previous chapters.

These are all additional conditions in addition to the fact of Jesus ontologically being both God and man. None of the above was possible without Christ living in the state of humiliation. In order for God to accomplish his goal to save men from his wrath He needed to satisfy his love and mercy without violating his justice. There was, according to God, no other way to do this. That is why he said his Son had to be **made** like his brethren, not the mere fact of being a human being in his nature.

3. Third Question

Could Christ keep the law as a perfect man without living at all times only as a man? Couldn't He live most of the time as a man, but part of the time as God?

The answer is, No. According to Scripture all men are born subject to the law of God and are compelled to obey it or suffer the consequences. So it is not just a matter of not sinning. And according to Scripture, Jesus was no exception. The consequence of failing to **keep** the law is the curse of eternal death. There is only one exception to this decree from God and that is if a man **did** live totally and completely according to the law of God, fulfilling all of its purposes. Then he could be accepted in the place of another as his substitute. Scripture says explicitly that Jesus was born **under** the law. Again we come back to Gal 4:4 "But when the fullness of time came, God sent forth his Son, born of a woman, born under the law," but The Holy Spirit goes on to say (v 5) "in order that He might redeem those who were under the law."

We must take care not to make human substitutions when we read Scripture. When Scripture declares that Christ must be "under the law" as a man, it is saying that He must at all times be under it, not merely that He must not break it! During the times He supposedly was given permission to act with his divine powers, exercising his divine attributes, He would certainly not be *breaking* the law, but it does mean that at those particular times He would not be **under** it. That would be contrary to what Scripture actually says.

And further, if it were possible for Jesus to be an exception to living his whole life by God's law or only part of the time fulfilling God's law or parts of God's law, it would be explicitly stated or even implied somewhere else in God's Holy Word. This is not found in Scripture. If we read in Scripture Christ was born under the law we must accept that statement from God at face value that in his life on earth He was **under** the law. There is no room for saying He was under the law part of the time as a human and part of the time as God the Son not under the law using omniscience, omnipotence, etc. How does that verse make any sense by reading into it that Christ was born under the law but did not need to live under the law in his life on earth, or that God gave Him an exemption to the law and lived it partially as the second person of the Trinity with all his divine Glory on display. If Christ was for any part of the time even with his Father's permission using his own divine power to fulfill part of the law, it could not be said of Him He handled his trials in the power of the Holy Spirit or by faith in God, as we have seen Scripture says in previous chapters, or that "we do not have a high priest who can not sympathize with our weaknesses, but one who has been tempted in all ways as we are, yet without sin"(Heb 4:15). Notice it says "in all ways," not all ways except where He was given an exemption. We submit that "in all ways" **means *in all ways!*** If Christ Jesus did not act fully as man exclusively, an exemption might be possible. The only other possibility is if He were part God and part man so that there could be an exception, but we have proven in Chapter 2 that He is fully God and fully man.

For Jesus to live part of his life as God also serves us no purpose. Ultimately God would be setting a different standard for his Son than He sets for us. Or maybe there are two different sets of laws, so maybe He didn't really mean his Son was under the law, or that his Son could redeem us some other way. All of this is convoluted and would require much speculation and conjecture to prove. But there is no need to speculate when the plain sense of Scripture is so clear:

First, we know Jesus did not violate the law by his own

declaration.

John 8:46 "Which one of you convicts Me of sin?"

Second, Scripture is clear that failure to **keep** the law in all points condemns:

James 2:10 ""For whoever keeps the whole law and yet stumbles in one point, he becomes guilty of all."

And to avoid the challenge and turn to using one's divine abilities instead of human abilities by faith would be to stumble in one point or many points. Moreover, it is as we said **keeping** the law as well as not sinning. Failing to do good is equal to sin.

James 4:17 Therefore to him that knoweth to do good, and doeth it not, to him it is sin.

Jesus did not fail to do good.

Third, God the Father was positively **pleased** with Christ.

Matt 17:5 "This is My beloved Son, in whom I am well pleased; And the Father continued to be pleased with his Son because Jesus **always** did the Father's will.

Fourth, Jesus knew He had to fulfill all righteousness from the start.

Matt 3:15 But Jesus answering said to him, "Permit it at this Time; for in this way it is fitting for us to fulfill all righteousness."

Matt 5:17 "Do not think that I came to abolish the law or the Prophets; but to fulfill."

These are not mere statements of not violating the law, but always keeping it.

Fifth, if Jesus missed any opportunity to fulfill any aspect of the law, ceremonial or moral law by the use of divine attributes, He would be guilty of using a crutch, or admitting it could not be done as a human. Gal 3:10 "For as many as are of the works of the Law are under a curse; for it is written, 'Cursed is everyone who does not abide by all things written in the book of the law, to perform them'." Again it is positive **performance** of **all** things in the law. Jesus had to perform all things as a man not as God. It was a matter not only of not violating the law but keeping it always. And here Scripture states it explicitly. Jesus as a man had to keep the law continually.

Sixth, Jesus fulfilled the law under his parents as well.

> Luke 2:21-27 "And when eight days were completed before His circumcision, His name was then called Jesus, the name given by the angel before He was conceived in the womb. 22. And when the days for their purification according to the Law of Moses were completed, they brought Him to Jerusalem to present Him to the Lord. 23. (As it is written in the law of the Lord, "Every first-born male that opens the womb shall be called Holy to the Lord"), 24. and to offer a sacrifice according to what was said in the law of the Lord"), "A pair of turtle doves, or two young pigeons."
>
> 27 And he came in the Spirit into the temple; and when the parents brought in the child Jesus, to carry out for Him the custom of the law.

Seventh, Jesus fulfilled the law to remove the requirement of believers having to obey all of it.

> Col 2:14 Having canceled out the certificate of debt consisting of decrees against us and which was hostile against us; and He has taken it out of the way, having nailed it to the cross.

That is paramount to an exclamation point, to the fact that Jesus lived all his life as a man obeying all the law of God.

Now the point of all this is to emphasize that in the state of his humiliation the Lord Jesus Christ lived exclusively and only at all times as a man, having emptied Himself of the use of all divine powers. And as we have continually stated it was by his own voluntary nonuse of them, never by not inherently having them.

But we feel constrained to look at it another way in what follows here.

Jesus in his humanity was exactly like us, except for sin. The Scripture did not resort to trickery when it said the Logos or the Son of God became man, as amazing as that statement is. The Holy God was Jesus' Father, and He had a righteous mother humanly speaking who had a sin nature and sinned just like us. In the Gospel of Luke her humanity is traced all the way back to Adam. Does that mean Jesus had a sin nature? Absolutely not. He was the holy child of

God Himself, who had no original sin imputed to Him at conception or birth, nor was it passed to him from his mother. He was without sin, and not merely without having sinned, but without a sin nature. Yet in order for Jesus to be in a position to offer Himself as a sacrifice to his Father in our place, He had to be like us in all things, but perfect, so that He could qualify to make propitiation for us and expiate our sin. On the other hand, merely being without sin does not make Him perfect for that purpose. We must remember from the preceding chapters that Scripture declares He was brought to perfection by the things He suffered. We are repeating this, because it is so essential to seeing how it relates to the question here.

> Heb 2:17 Therefore, He had to be made like His brethren in all things, that He might become a merciful and faithful high priest in things pertaining to God, to make propitiation for the sins of the people.

We must emphasize again that making propitiation for the sins of the people **required** that He be made like his brethren in all things, not just being human but in a human life in order to become a merciful and faithful high priest.

> Heb 9:26 At the consummation of the ages He has been manifested to put away sin by the sacrifice of Himself.

> Mark 10:45 For even the Son of man did not come to be served, but to serve, and to give His life a ransom for many.

> 1 John 3:5 And you know that He appeared in order to take away sins; and in Him there is no sin.

There are many passages of Scripture which say the same thing as these four verses. The Bible affirms that Jesus came to die as a sacrifice for the salvation of all who would come to Him.

In the history of the church this has always been emphasized. For example, the Heidelberg Catechism asks: Question 16 "Why must He be a true and sinless man?" Answer: "Because the justice of God requires that the same human nature which had sinned should make satisfaction for sin; but no man, being himself a sinner, could satisfy for others." Of course the imputation of sin in general and our sins in particular to Jesus came at the end of his life. (2 Cor

5:21; Isaiah 53:6)

But now as time has passed renewed attention needs to be given to the same truth. The emphasis on his humanity in the preceding chapters in no way denies or impugns his deity. On the contrary, God is glorified when extolling the proper balance of the God-Man. When proper attention is given to all the Old Testament prophesies concerning God's Son, He was God of very God who in order to fulfill all of God's plans had to be made like his brethren in every way, man of very man. Jesus had to fulfill all of God's law without using any of his divine powers to accomplish his complete obedience to the law.

The bottom line answer to the third question here is: In order for Jesus to make propitiation and be an acceptable sacrifice to God to atone for our sins his humanity needs to be understood as we have shown in the above chapters. The way in which Jesus' sacrifice made an acceptable atonement to God for our sins needs to be considered. Christ was our substitute. As a substitute He had both to be human and live a perfect life.

The doctrine of Christ as our substitute embraces the element of a benefit for the recipient. When the Greek word *anti* is used separately or in compound words it implies strict substitution. When *huper* is used it usually means Christ died in the sinner's place and for the sinner's benefit. In any event, the truths that Christ's death was substitutionary and that it was beneficial in nature are well established.

This is only a sampling of the biblical fact that Christ died vicariously or in place of sinners, and it positively affirms Jesus is our substitute and the One who was qualified and who willingly died in our place. The above also suggests and should not be overlooked that the One who was righteous and sinless came for the benefit of the unrighteous and the sinful.

4. Fourth Question

How do we understand what Scripture says concerning

131

sacrifice in connection with the actual salvation of people consistent with the truths of the preceding chapters?

On the one hand Christ by his death made a perfect substitutionary sacrifice for sins. But Christ's righteousness has to connect with individual people. This takes place by God's act of justifying repentant believing sinners. So an account must be given how that takes place, and how the life of Christ relates to that justification. This is the other side of the atonement. How individual people are brought into God's presence as well as how it was made possible.

In order for a person to enter God's throne room, an individual must be sinless and completely righteous. This needs to be understood biblically. God does not just require that a person be sinless, but that he has lived a perfect life. We have seen how that relates to what Christ accomplished on earth.

First, God is holy and righteous, and according to the prophet Habakkuk 1:13, "He is of purer eyes than to behold evil and He can not look upon iniquity," and it is a fact that not one of us is righteous according to Paul in Rom 3:10-23. So how is it that we as Christians can enter boldly into God's presence without being consumed on the spot? We already know that Christ's sacrifice was substitutionary on our behalf, and covers all our sins, so much so, that our sins are forgiven past, present, and future, "as far as the east is from the west." But where does our righteousness come from so that God sees us as not only sinless but as completely righteous? It is derived from Christ's humanity. Before a righteous life can be imputed to anyone, someone, a man, must have lived that perfect righteous life - a whole life from birth to death. Scripture says that Jesus came to fulfill the whole law and to fulfill all righteousness (Gal 4:4-5; Matt 3:15).

God could **not** just impute his own divine righteousness directly to us; it had to be earned by a perfect substitute, one who had attained perfection, human perfection, meeting every standard of God's perfection. 2 Cor 5:21 "He made Him who knew no sin to be sin on our behalf, that we might become the righteousness of God in Him." We have the privilege to enter into Christ's righteousness, but remember that it was not due to his sinlessness which He was born with, but that it was righteousness acquired and earned through his life of keeping the law always doing good. We must abandon the attitude of having all of our sins forgiven as the only thing that needs to be considered.

We come to God not having any righteousness of our own but can only receive the benefit of Christ's righteousness to qualify us to enter into the throne room of God. That righteousness is a positional righteousness that we have before God by virtue only of our connection with Christ. Practical righteousness is something else completely, that comes by running the race of faith as Jesus did, allowing the Holy Spirit to transform us into the image of the Lord just as we encounter his glories in the mirror of Scripture as it is applied to life. So indeed in our salvation, more is needed than only positional righteousness. But positional righteousness takes care of everything about our standing before God, permanently. Yes, Christ is also our example for our sanctification, which is taken up in the next chapter.

8.

IMPLICATIONS OF
THE DOCTRINE OF SANCTIFICATION
FOR CHRIST'S HUMANITY

The believer's sanctification is one of the two reasons God leaves us here in this world after we have received the Holy Spirit and have been regenerated and placed into the body of Christ. The other reason is to preach the gospel to all peoples. And when Christ's church has the right motive, pursuing these endeavors all three persons of the Trinity are glorified. So with that in mind, the sanctification process is of utmost importance to every believer that is truly saved, to the end that we be holy and blameless before Him in love!

There are a number of things we need to understand concerning the process of our sanctification if we are to please God. In this chapter we concern ourselves particularly with the importance of Christ's humanity and how it relates to our being conformed to him. The Holy Spirit has been given to the believer for that purpose and to empower each one not only to fulfill their particular task in the church but also to become complete in Christ.

What is meant by the term sanctification? We know from Scripture that the English word sanctification is translated from roots of the Greek *hagiasmos* and Hebrew *qodesh*, and has different meanings according to its use, whether it is used as a noun, adjective, or verb. And using either of these it is further defined by the scriptural context. The literal root meaning is separateness or dedication. God is holy because He is separate from everything else in glory and majesty. People are holy basically because they are separated and dedicated to God to serve Him. Objects are holy when dedicated and separated for exclusive use in serving God.

Sanctification must be understood as having two sides. There is positional sanctification and practical sanctification. Positional sanctification means being separated to God. Positional sanctification relates to the way

God looks at Christians apart from what they actually are morally. Practical sanctification takes place as a person becomes set apart to God in the way he lives. And that, of course, begins when God transforms a person by regeneration.

What we will attempt to do is show how the human life of Christ has relevance in both positional and practical sanctification. They both imply the correct view of Christ's humanity.

Positional Sanctification

All Christians are called Saints or holy by the Holy Spirit (Rom 1:7, 1 Cor 1:2, Eph 1:1, Phil 1:1 Col 1:1, etc). This means fundamentally that God calls and sets aside people out of the world and consecrates them to Himself. They are his and they are set aside for his purpose. And all of this is made possible by the life and works of Christ and applied by the Holy Spirit.

> 1 Cor 1:2 To the church of God which is at Corinth, to those who have been sanctified in Christ Jesus, saints by calling, with all who in every place call upon the name of our Lord Jesus Christ, their Lord and ours.

> Acts 26:18 Among those who have been sanctified by faith in Me.

Sanctification is stated as already having taken place in Corinth, but it was a church that was definitely not sanctified in practice. This is positional sanctification. The word *saints* literally means holy ones, from the Greek root *hag-*, just like sanctification and holiness. So people are looked on as holy by God because of their connection with Christ. In referring to a person having a position before God because of his union or connection with Christ, it can be called "positional sanctification" or "positional holiness." That is a kind of parallel to "positional justification" or "positional righteousness." But these two are not synonymous.

Positional sanctification occurs by connection with Christ.

God sees us **in** Christ, seeing Him instead of us, when He sees us.

Positional sanctification does not take place in isolation from the work of God within those who believe. Who He sees in Christ are also transformed by the regenerating work of the Spirit of God.

Practical Sanctification.

According to Scripture, when one is fully sanctified he or she will be like Christ. It is one of the greatest promises from God. What a thought, that God promises that all of us believers will be conformed to the image of Christ! But what does God mean by his promise? Let us not try to analyze why God wants to conform us to the image of his Son, but let us realize what the part was that Jesus contributed to our sanctification, and what exactly is expected of us and what our contribution will be. Practical sanctification is a process whereby believers are being consecrated and separated to God and become holy as God is holy. And this is a process that continues throughout life.

How it works out is through a number of realities in our lives in addition to what is true positionally. Col 3:8-12 says that since we have laid aside the old self and have put on the new self, we are to put on a heart of compassion. And Eph 3:2 says we were by nature children of wrath, but God made us alive in Christ. And Rom 6:13 tells us not to go on presenting the members of our bodies to sin as instruments of unrighteousness, but to present ourselves to God as those alive from the dead. And Rom 12:1-3 says to present our bodies a living sacrifice to God and be transformed by the renewing of our minds. All of this is explained as being made possible by the Holy Spirit who empowers a person to put to death the deeds of the body of flesh (Rom 8:13). So God sets a person apart positionally, and makes changes within so that practical sanctification becomes possible.

In order to bring practical sanctification about, the believer needs to do certain things: (1) be filled with the Spirit, (2) understand the goal (renewal of mind, etc.), (3) walk by faith, (4) in faith overcome the flesh, and (5) see the example of Christ accurately and have a true vision of Him – "walk as He walked." It is beyond the scope of this book to go into the details of sanctification. The concern is to show how Christ's life contributes to the believer's sanctification.

Here are biblical passages which show the necessity of practical sanctification:

Eph 1:4 God chose us in him before the foundation of the world, that we should be holy and blameless before him in love.

1 Peter 1:15 But like the Holy One who called you, be holy yourselves also in all your behavior; v 16 because it is written, "you shall be holy for I am holy."

These are not statements about positional sanctification, which is true of all believers, but of practical sanctification.

Now, what does Scripture say about practical sanctification in relation to Jesus?

Heb 12:1-2 Let us also lay aside every encumbrance, and the sin which so easily entangles us, and let us run with endurance the race that is set before us, v 2 fixing our eyes on Jesus, the author and perfecter of faith, who for the joy set before him endured the cross, despising the shame, and has sat down at the right hand of the throne of God.

1 Peter 2:21 For you have been called for this purpose, since Christ also suffered for you, leaving you an example for you to follow in his steps.

Having Jesus as an example for us to follow and not have the correct view of his humanity would be self-defeating. It would be very frustrating to say the least. Since our sanctification is such an important part of the remaining time each of us has left here in this world this process needs to be understood. We will again follow the method of asking and answering questions, as in other chapters.

1. First Question

Could the statement that Jesus was tested in all points as we are, be fulfilled without living his whole life as a man, the God-Man?

The answer comes from Heb 4:15 "For we do not have a high priest who can not sympathize with our weaknesses, but one who has been tempted in all things as we are, yet without sin." If Jesus lived his life and did signs and wonders by his own power and then told the apostles they would do even more than He did, but they would need to live in uninterrupted faith, calling on the power of the Holy Spirit for life and miracles, wouldn't that be a contradiction to this verse which would border hypocrisy? Scripture could not make the claim that He was tempted in all things as we are if He wasn't tempted as we are, but rather was tempted as the incarnate God the Son using his divine abilities to meet the temptation. We do not have divine powers to call on, so if Jesus used them, that would be wholly **unlike** us. Never having seen God yet we believe and we call on God's intervention, but that is not using divine powers that we do not have. So He would not be an example for us of withstanding temptation unless like us in that respect. It is true He was tempted in all things as we are, and that is very comforting. It's also comforting to know Jesus did not fall back and count on his divine powers in difficult situations.

2. Second Question

Could Christ be our example for our sanctification by living part of his life acting as God using his divine powers?

If Jesus lived only part of his life without using his divine powers, who would we ask for clarification on how much omniscience, and so forth for each of his attributes, he used and how often he used it? And wouldn't that be a fair question since Scripture says He acted by the power of the Holy Spirit and not in his own power of omniscience, and so forth? There is no biblical principle available to us which we could employ when we attempt to interpret the details of Christ's life seeking to gain insight on this accurately from the word of God for our sanctification. Theologians are the ones who have been telling us for more than a century now that Jesus set aside during his state of humiliation only the free and independent exercise of his divine powers, but actually used them according as his Father gave Him permission. This thought translates to God the Son, the Lord

138

Jesus Christ, not emptying Himself but rather actually using his divine attributes on earth to enable Him to fulfill all righteousness. By extension He therefore **did** act by his own divine powers and not in the power of the Holy Spirit and not by faith at particular points in his life. We have been told this only for the last one hundred and twenty years. Prior to that, we are told that theology simply said that Jesus did not use his divine attributes during his humiliation. It is an innovation in the articulation of doctrine as far as we know. However, long before this, theologians mostly interpreted passages of Scripture as Christ using his divine powers. And no mention is made of being given permission. But we now would have to ask the question about this permission. When was He given this permission, if He was given permission from the Father, to use his divine power? Was it all the time? How would we ever know since the Bible never ever says anything about Him being given permission to use his divine power? It is all drawn out of thin air!

3. Third Question

Is Christ our example of suffering in order for us to bear our own cross?

In order to be conformed to Christ's image there is another element which should be explored and is also an important part of the sanctification process. It is not enough to be conformed to Christ's image of holiness and righteousness, but also his image of affliction and suffering. How do we know that? From Scripture:

> Col 1:24 Now I rejoice in my sufferings for your sake, and in my flesh I do my share on behalf of His body (which is the church) in filling up that which is lacking in Christ's afflictions.

Paul who was in prison when writing Colossians was taking the afflictions meant for Christ since they could not directly punish Christ any longer. So they vented their anger on Paul. This suggests Paul's gradual filling up of the afflictions to come.

> Phil 3:7-14 But whatever things were gain to me, those things I have counted as loss for the sake of Christ. 8. More than that I count all things to be loss in view of knowing Christ Jesus my Lord, for whom I have suffered the loss of all things, and count them but rubbish in order that I may gain Christ, 9. and may be

found in Him, not having a righteousness of my own derived from the law, but that which is through faith in Christ, the righteousness which comes from God on the basis of faith; 10. that I may know Him, and the power of His resurrection, and the fellowship of His sufferings, being conformed to His death, 11. in order that I may attain to the resurrection from the dead.

Paul continues on and is pressing Toward the Goal

Phil 3:12 Not that I have already obtained it, or have already become perfect; but I press on in order that I may lay hold of that for which also I was laid hold of by Christ Jesus. 13. Brethren, I do not regard myself as having laid hold of it; but one thing I do: forgetting what lies behind and reaching forward to what lies ahead, 14. I press on toward the goal for the prize of the upward call of God in Christ Jesus.

The Apostle Paul is a great example for us to follow, but listen also to what the Apostle Peter has to say.

1 Peter 2:21 For to this you were called, because Christ also suffered for us, leaving us an example, that you should follow His steps.

1 Peter 4:1 Therefore, since Christ suffered for us in the flesh, arm yourselves also with the same mind, for he who has suffered in the flesh has ceased from sin.

1 Peter 5:8-11 Be sober; be vigilant, because your adversary the devil walks about like a roaring lion, seeking whom he may devour. 9. Resist him, steadfast in the faith, knowing that the same sufferings are experienced by your brotherhood in the world. 10. But may the God of all grace, who called us to his eternal glory by Christ Jesus, after you have suffered a while, perfect, establish, strengthen, and settle you. 11. To Him be the glory and the dominion forever and ever. Amen.

There are too many Scriptures which tell us we should be suffering for Christ as we are molded in his image to mention them all, but just one more is appropriate to affirm this necessary part of our sanctification. If sufferings were what conformed Jesus to the image of God we should travel the same path as He did. Jesus warned us that we would suffer for Him:

John 15:18 If the world hated you, you know that it hated Me before it hated you. 19. If you were of the world, the world would love its own; but because you are not of the world, but I chose you out of the world, therefore the world hates you 20. Remember the word that I said to you, "A slave is not greater than his master." If they persecuted Me, they will also persecute you;

Jesus when praying to the Father said something very similar:

> John 17:14-19 I have given them thy word; and the world has hated them, because they are not of the world, even as I am not of the world. 15. I do not ask Thee to take them out of the world, but to keep them from the evil one. 16. They are not of the world even as I am not of the world. 17. Sanctify them in the truth; Thy word is truth. 18. As Thou didst send Me into the world, I also have sent them into the world. 19. And for their sakes I sanctify Myself, that they themselves also may be sanctified in truth.

We should be getting the picture that the sanctification process includes our suffering just like Jesus and his apostles endured. Peter accused his own countrymen of murdering the innocent Savior! Jesus cleansed the temple with a whip and talked more about hell than He did about heaven.

The failure to suffer for our sanctification stems from, at least in large part because of our misunderstanding the real and true humanity of our Savior. He was and is a man's man. He was not a wimp or a milk toast. It takes a real man to stand up to this system we live in, so let's not forget the millions of women and their love and passion for Jesus who were and are today being tortured and killed for their Savior. And they are by and large ignored by Christians in America! Why? Because Christians here are fearful to take even a modicum of criticism from the world! All it takes is obedience to Christ who doesn't ask us to do anything He didn't suffer and doing it all through walking in and being filled with the Holy Spirit. Justin Martyr's words which he penned before he was executed with six others goes something like this: "you can hate and despise us and hurt and torture us, and you can kill us, but I thank God you can't do us any real harm." That is paraphrased since it has been heard quoted in various ways. But the message is still the same. Justin knew Jesus to be a man as He is portrayed in the Scriptures and he knew Jesus never called on his divine powers to help Himself out of a difficult trial, especially not during at anytime in the last week of his life or for that matter at any other time in his life.

141

The Epistle to the Hebrews says it best: Heb 2:18 "For since He himself was tempted in that which He has suffered, He is able to come to the aid of those who are tempted." Heb 5:8 "Although He was a Son, He learned obedience from the things which He suffered." Heb 2:10 "For it was fitting for Him, for whom are all things, and through whom are all things, in bringing many sons to glory, to perfect the author of their salvation through sufferings."

There is no question the Apostles are our example and that Jesus is our supreme example, and if they were sanctified through sufferings where does that leave us? Isn't it the perspective of Jesus in his severe words:

> Luke 9:23-24 And He was saying to them all, "If anyone wishes to come after Me, let him deny himself, and take up his cross daily, and follow Me."

What Jesus was saying to those who wanted to follow Him was they would suffer daily as Jesus was doing, and that was the cross they would need to bear. The suffering would continue daily and while the trials would not stop, the Apostle Paul tells us "No temptation has over-taken you but such as is common to man; and God is faithful, who will not allow you to be tempted beyond what you are able, but with the temptation will provide the way of escape also, that you may be able to endure it" (1 Cor 10:13).

4. Fourth Question

In the process of being sanctified how does Christ's life compare with the Christian life?

Granted that Christ at all points was tested as a man without the use of his divine powers, and granted that Christ was our example for our sanctification without using his divine powers, and granted that He was our example of suffering in order for us to bear our own cross. Beyond being our example, He is also our vision. We are sanctified by more than our own following Him as our example.

> 2 Cor 3:18 But we all, with unveiled face beholding as in a mirror the glory of the Lord, are being transformed into the same image from glory to glory, just as from the Lord, the Spirit.

This passages shows that we are transformed by the correct

vision of Christ. Many interpret this passage as seeing the splendor of Christ's **divine** glory in the mirror. However, it is impossible to interpret this passage accurately without the proper doctrine of Christ's humanity, since it is mostly his humanity we are seeing in the mirror. Yet nearly every biblical commentary says its Christ's divine glory we are seeing in the mirror. That is far from the truth according to the Scripture. All we have to do is look at what the words of the passage say. They do not say that we are transformed into a divine image! They say that we are transformed into the **same** image. It is impossible for the same image in us to be the divine Glory of God! The **only** image possible for us to be transformed into is the human image of the God-Man. But that image that we do see is the full human image of Christ, perfected through a process that led to his glorification. Hence, the image is the image of the same progress in us that Christ Himself experienced. This is a staggering thought. He is the pattern for us, not just by way of example, but as a tremendous vision.

The divine Son of God became a man and what you see on display in the Bible is his humanity and rarely his divinity. But we are not to think of Jesus acting in his humanity apart from his divinity. He acts as a person. Nevertheless as a person He acts as a man, now an exalted man. Even in the book of Revelation, highly exalted, He appears as a glorified being, a glorified man receiving revelation from God the Father! We have seen Christ's humility on display in his preincarnate existence in which He voluntarily humbles Himself. He was in the form of God and equal to God. But when He became a man He learned humility, not born with it, just like He learned every other godly virtue, always by faith and in the power of the Holy Spirit.

We would all agree that Jesus was and is one hundred percent man but where the error comes in is with the implications of what this means. For instance, no man can change water to wine, walk on water, calm a storm, raise a dead person, heal diseases, or cast out demons, unless either he was other than a real man, or else of course God was with him.

When we behold the glory of the Lord as in a mirror,

humility is one of the very first things we should see. If we leave the mirror unaffected or unmoved by his humility, and do not understand exactly what that means to teach each one of us, we should be ashamed, and immediately ask for forgiveness. We have in the apostles a great sense of humility, but to see humility in full display, you will need to behold it in the Lord as in a mirror, discerning how this is evident or even possible in the Lord's life, and by comparison make application to our own life. This is true of all of the other virtues and glories of Christ as well. If you are aware of this process, aided by the Spirit in the life of the Son of man, you will find it being produced in your own life even by the Spirit of Christ.

True sanctification involves seeing Jesus for who He really is as outlined in the preceding chapters, and when this is done, being conformed to the glory of Christ becomes on our part, natural. Out of love we obey his commands and his commandments are not burdensome and He gives us the increase of faith we need and desire; it is no longer we who live but Christ who lives in us.

In conclusion it must be said that positional sanctification because it is an act of God and will continue to be bestowed upon regenerated sinners as it was in Corinth, but as for practical sanctification unless a change is implemented Christ's church will continue on without its greatest weapon, the full example and vision of its leader Jesus Christ himself. The Spirit is speaking from his Word clearly to each of us, to teach and extol the full virtues of Christ's humanity. Both positional and practical sanctification depend on our proper connection to Jesus Christ our Savior and brother who is Prophet, Priest, and King.

9.

CONCLUSION

In the history of the Christian church believers have always held that Christ Jesus was true God and true man. However, the implications of this fundamental truth has been obscured time and again. True Christians have to be on continual guard against human thinking that can cause confusion and undermine faith. The great deceiver, Satan, has multiplied counterfeits for every kind of human personality, cultural variation, and intellectual climate. This is true in the area of theology as well as false church fellowships and Christian practice. The thesis of this book relates to an area of doctrine that has never been addressed in the Bible-believing church of the Lord Jesus Christ.

There is clear acknowledgment of fundamental Christology, stated forcefully in the early Church at the Council of Chalcedon, and believed by true Christians from the beginning though not articulated with precision. And later when German Rationalism infected theology and spread far and wide, deviations were recognized and soundly rejected.

But on the thesis of this book there has never been a straightforward and consistent treatment that by all rights **ought** to have been done a very, very long time ago. Instead, biblical passages concerning the events in the life of Jesus have been interpreted piecemeal without consideration of the overall teaching of Scripture concerning his life on earth during the state of his self-humiliation to accomplish our eternal salvation. Rather, even the best expositors and theologians have followed what others have said before and interpreted these events in terms of the use of Jesus' divine abilities despite hints and evidence to the contrary.

This book has shown that Jesus lived entirely as a man based on the positive teaching of Scripture, which gives the necessary, normative and regulative presumption that He never ever, not even once, used his divine abilities. In addition, the book gives a clear reason why He might do that. And on this basis, upon examination of the events where Jesus might be thought to have used his divine abilities, completely **adequate** explanations have been adduced on considerations drawn directly from Scripture itself. Then, a correct understanding of the roles of Jesus as Prophet, Priest and Sacrifice, and the fact that Jesus is an example for believers for their sanctification - these confirm that the thesis developed in the preceding chapters is not only possible, but entirely **necessary**.

10.

EPILOGUE

Much of what has been discussed will be difficult to digest, and we say that with great understanding. We are so intimately involved with the Lord Jesus Christ that to be shown any error in how we perceive Him will cause the soul some degree of shock. We are in touch with Him everyday all day in our own individual way; He means more to us than our church and family members.

We have been careful not to demean other authors and the many theologians down through the centuries who have interpreted Scripture contrary to what they themselves correctly believe concerning the humanity of Jesus Christ the God-Man. In short, they have been inconsistent. But in propounding the truth of Him these errors will inevitably come to the surface. This author has been told many times including people with good intentions that focusing on the subject of Christ's humanity with any amount of intensity somehow detracts from or denies Christ's deity. In fact, leaders in the church have charged me with having a one-track mind and making this truth a hobby-horse. And they say that in reality overly concentrating on our Savior's life is unnecessary. They contradict Ps 40:7 and Heb 10:7.

The truth is that the reality of the true person and work of the Lord Jesus Christ is at the very foundation of all of our Christian doctrines, from the time of creation, salvation, and to the final state. If any student of Scripture misunderstands the real biblical facts surrounding Christ's person and work, his studies will be impeded. The motive of our work has been to please God by knowing him more accurately and to be ready to give an answer to everyone who asks the reason of our hope which is grounded in Jesus Christ his Son. Every Christian should be concerned about this. It is not a minor issue. We have detailed biblically the facts surrounding the ontology of Jesus Christ that in his being he is both fully God and fully man, but we have also declared the significance of this truth and how it works out in our lives. We have elaborated the truths of Christ's humanity, but not at the expense of his deity, keeping them in proper balance. The actions of our Savior are just as important as who He is in his Person. That alone is what we have addressed in this book. The average Christian will have no difficulty with the content. The problem arises mainly due to prejudice that arises from traditional thinking both in academic study of theology and scholarly expositions of Scripture.

By understanding the biblical truths about Jesus' life on earth we will be able to answer any questions arising from his life as recorded in the gospels. The mystery of the incarnation will not completely be solved, but the unnecessary mystery that has come out of confusion surrounding his self-humiliation is solved.

There are many great men and woman in my fellowship from my pastor to the man (Edgar) who sweeps the floors. I am sure they love Christ as I do. A number of great theologians whose works I have read and assimilated down through the years have all influenced me, and it is much appreciated. Why I have been led to write this book is still a mystery to me, even after the many times I sought an answer in prayer.

I make no apology for taking a different approach to interpreting the life of our Christ, even though in reality I believe the difference in doctrinal expression is slight. But the implications of what has been said here are profoundly different from the current traditional view. Jesus is not pleased with how his church presently views and presents Him, and He wants these changes we have discussed implemented as soon as possible. I have awakened from sleep many times that what I have written here needs to be done. All who have studied to show themselves approved or who are somewhere in that process will agree Jesus is one hundred percent God and one hundred percent man, but then we interpret and view Him with an emphasis on his deity rather than seeing Him for who He really is, equally God and man - The Christ of God, truly our Savior our King and our brother.

APPENDIX A

CAUSE OF THE CURRENT CONFUSION

"The Logos voluntarily gave up the *independent* exercise of his divine attributes."

There needs to be an explanation for the most current and very popular error concerning Christ Jesus the Son of God. Whatever the explanation is it needs to be exposed and defeated. It isn't as though God offers us a number of kenosis options to choose from because when He communicates his thoughts his meanings are quite clear. Those who promulgated this incorrect theory of Christ's self-emptying doctrine have been very sincere followers of Christ, and also very credible and distinguished. But why did it start and where and when did it start and for that matter with whom did it start?

We will attempt to unravel why it started, by acknowledging from history the heretical Kenoticists, and the part they played. According to Dorner, the Kenoticists began their persuasion of Christ's self-emptying in the early seventeen hundreds. They taught in one degree or another that Christ in some way gave up all or some of his divine attributes when becoming a man. From the early church all the way through the reformers this error of the Kenoticists was never taught, so we may assume from the first Kenoticists it was advanced by Thomasius in 1853. We may only surmise this brought on a reaction to the point of outrage among sound theologians. This probably caused a line to be drawn in the sand, and the many who denounced the Kenoticist's error of Christ's person and works perhaps moved too quickly to respond. Such was the case when the deity of Christ was defended so vigorously over the centuries and is even today defended so as to do so at the expense of his humanity. But we cannot excuse the overreaction because the sin involved is perpetrated against God Himself. The correct balance is to be found in God's Holy Word. Sadly, too many feel the need to pontificate on every word of the Bible even when they were not called or empowered to do so. Many of the greatest among us from the early church to the current church have weighed in on subjects that should have been left alone when they should have confessed lack of clear understanding. If so, maybe the church would be farther along in its evangelism and sanctification. The gates of hell will not prevail but it may be giving us some trouble we need to identify and defeat.

Where the latest lack of understanding of the person and work of Christ started is very interesting. Of all places who would have guessed that it was right here in the United States of America, and regrettably during the end of a wave of the great awakening. As far as we have been able to determine with the limited resources available to us, it started in the eighteen hundreds when the church was booming here in America.

According to A. H. Strong, orthodoxy was, up until his time, *not* that Christ voluntarily gave up the independent exercise of divine attributes, but that He very simply gave up the exercise of his divine attributes. The word "*independent*" was added without thinking through the implications and that it changes one's entire view of what Christ did. This interpretation of adding the word *independent* leads to contradiction after contradiction, to the point of making it difficult if not impossible to make sense of significant parts of Christ's life. What happened ultimately was the true glory of his person has been confused and hidden.

Where it happened in America is even more interesting; it came from academia, by a truly credible theologian, president and professor of theological studies of a prominent seminary, having the designation of Doctor of Divinity. Why, where, and when are not as important as to who started this trend. And what is just as important is that Christians are willing to go along with it without checking to see if it accords with the Scripture. Amazingly enough, many who follow along are enthusiastic dedicated students of God's Holy Word. Seminary is quite intimidating because one is taught by some of the most gifted men in the church. The church needs more Bereans who are truly not worried of the outcome when speaking up or just asking questions. The Bereans checked up on an Apostle commissioned by Christ Himself! So, how much more should we be cautious and discerning, with regard to the pronouncement of those who are not Apostles? Note that the Apostle Paul declared that "we are helpers," not authorities with dominion over one's faith.

> 2 Cor 1:24 Not for that we have dominion over your faith, but are helpers of your joy: for by faith ye stand.

As far as can be found the present articulation of Christ's ministry came from A.H. Strong.

Augustus Hopkins Strong President of Rochester Theological Seminary, born Aug. 3, 1836 graduated Yale College 1857, was converted to Christianity while in college. He began theological studies at Rochester Theological Seminary, completed his D.D. in Germany. In August 1861 he was ordained pastor of First Baptist Church, Haverhill, MA. In 1865 he became pastor of First Church Cleveland, OH. He became president of Rochester Theological Seminary in 1872 and his tenure lasted forty years. (The Rochester Theological Seminary is now called Colgate Rochester Divinity School in Rochester.) During his time at Rochester he received several distinguished degrees including a D.D. degree from Brown, Yale, and Princeton, and a Lit. Degree from University of Rochester. He also served on the board of trusties at Vassar College, and from 1907 to 1910 he served as first president of the Northern Baptist Convention; now called the American Baptist Churches in U. S. A. Dr. Strong died in Pasadena, California in 1921.

It is said that Dr. Strong preferred the orthodox Lutheran European theologies to the American because he detected in the former thoroughness and comprehensiveness in handling problems of understanding, while in the latter he did not. As to the doctrine of election, Dr. Strong was an advocate of the moderate-Calvinistic "Sublapsarian" view. He mostly wrote from a committed Reformed and Baptist perspective. Dr. Strong believed Christ's second coming was premillennial but postmillennial physically and visibly. These two views were not in conflict in Strong's mind.

Strong was comfortable with the idea that God may have created the world through the process of evolution. In the 1907 edition of his theology, Strong summarized his views on modern thought: "Neither evolution nor higher criticism has any terrors to one who regards them as part of Christ's creating and education process."

It is said of Dr. Strong he held to orthodox Evangelical theology.

In 1886, while President of the seminary, Dr. Strong had his most celebrated work published, his **Systematic Theology**. This work was well received in its time and has continued to be highly recommended in Christian circles to this day. We believe Dr. Strong introduced an innovation.

When A. H. Strong added the word "*independent*" to his interpretation of Christ's self-emptying of Himself, he made a very significant change. In this regard he himself distinguished what he was saying from "old orthodoxy." So he admits leaving this "old orthodoxy," at least in his doctrine of Christ's humiliation, Christ's kenosis.

Dr. Strong admits in point #4 below that his theory is not "Old Orthodoxy." So as far as we have been able to trace, A. H. Strong began what is now referred to as "the traditional view," which according to what he said was not the traditional view until he launched it in 1886, approximately one hundred twenty five years ago.

From **Systematic Theology** 1886, page 382 we quote:

"Our doctrine of Christ's humiliation will be better understood, if we put it midway between two pairs of erroneous views, making it the third of five. The list would be as follows: (1) Gess: The Logos gave up all divine attributes; (2) Thomasius: The Logos gave up relative attributes only; (3) True view; The Logos gave up the independent exercise of divine attributes; (4) Old Orthodoxy: Christ gave up the use of divine attributes; (5) Anselm: Christ acted as if He did not possess divine attributes.

Numbers (1) and (2) are two of the false teachings of the Kenoticists mentioned in Chapter 2 and Appendix B, which are to be entirely rejected. (3) Strong was mistaken in saying that "Old Orthodoxy" asserted that Christ gave up the use of divine attributes. Older interpreters state that Christ did in fact in his state of humiliation use his own divine powers and that they were a demonstration of his deity. But what Strong states as "Old Orthodoxy" is what we actually see in the Bible.

151

Strong offers his interpretation as a theory:

"That the humiliation consisted in the surrender of the independent exercise of divine attributes. This *theory* (emphasis added) which we regard as the most satisfactory of all, may be more fully set forth as follows: The humiliation, as the scriptures seem to show, consisted:

(a) In that act of the preexistent Logos by which he gave up his divine glory with the Father, in order to take a servant form. In this act, He resigned not the possession, nor yet entirely the use, but rather the independent exercise, of the divine attributes.

(b) In the submission of the Logos to the control of the Holy Spirit and the limitations of his Messianic mission, in his communication of the divine fullness to the human nature which He had taken into union with Himself.

(c) In the continuous surrender, on the part of the God-man, so far as his human nature was concerned, of the exercise of those divine powers, with which it was endowed by virtue of its union with the divine, and in the voluntary acceptance, which followed upon this, of temptation, suffering, and death."

We may comment on what Strong said. With respect to point (a), Jesus retained his glory; He did not give it up as Strong said. Rather He gave up the public display of his inherent glory which He retained. And He truly did not give up the possession of any divine attributes, as Strong says, but did give up their use, and did so voluntarily so that they were not available. Strong denies this last, but gives lip-service to giving up some use of them. With regard to point (b) it propounds the wrong idea of the Lutherans that Strong adopted at this point that divinity was *communicated* to the human nature! But Strong is right that Jesus did submit to the control of the Holy Spirit with regard to his Messianic mission. But what Strong failed to see is that his Messianic mission required him to fulfill a complete human life, so that his whole life would be subject to that control. And with regard to point (c) Strong repeats the Lutheran error, but is right in saying He surrendered the exercise of his divine powers! Yet then he contradicts himself, in a way followed by virtually all theologians after him, by making an exception found nowhere in Scripture, that God gives Him permission to use them.

Let's clarify that the word *independent* here has nothing to do with the inter-Trinitarian relations. It has only to do with Christ in his Messianic mission. Within the Trinity the three members of God act independently but nevertheless in complete agreement and harmony. This does not justify introducing the word *independent* in the way Strong does. It is not inter-Trinitarian actions that are at issue, but the voluntary decision of God the Son, deciding independently to give up the mere **use** of his divine abilities. Saying that He gave up the independent use simply declares that He didn't do what He decided to do. And it involves God the Father and God the Son in rejecting the choice of God the Son, and themselves making exceptions to it. So it in reality implies a disharmony in the Trinity. God the Son chooses one thing and the other members choose to override it and tell the Son to use his own divine powers against the choice of the Son.

The continuing problem the church is faced with is taking the church leaders back to the Bible. We have chosen not to identify in this work the credible theologians who have taken the baton from Dr. Strong and run with it. The list of teachers and theologians we had compiled was long and quite distinguished. But it is enough that their work is exposed to the light of Scripture, no matter how outstanding otherwise, especially in articulating the truths concerning the Trinity and the incarnation.

It is an easy sell to preach Christ Jesus in all his splendor working his many miracles in his own power, but his humanity is eclipsed in the process and the church will be the worse for it. I am sure He is not happy with what his church has allowed to be said about Himself and wants it to change directions now. Remember that God's wrath was kindled against Job's friends for misrepresenting Him and I'm sure this same wrath has been rekindled. If so, in line with 2 John 8, which is a warning to Christians, they can lose their rewards for not understanding what Christ's coming in the flesh means. I believe it includes his walk on earth as well as his incarnation.

APPENDIX B

KENOTICISM

It is important to understand Kenoticism and how it differs entirely from the teaching of Scripture about Christ's self-emptying. Kenoticism is the heretical view that as part of the incarnation in order to enter his state of humiliation the divine Logos gave up some or all of his inherent divine attributes. That means that in the incarnation Christ was ontologically not completely God. The biblical view is that in the incarnation Christ did not give up any inherent divine attributes and was ontologically fully God, but that He gave up the use of divine abilities or attributes and that alone.

The errors of the Kenotic Theologians are similar and in one form or another they promulgate that Christ gave up or emptied Himself of his inherent divine attributes in order to become a man. It started by asserting that Christ emptied Himself of only his relative attributes or noncommunicable attributes: omnipotence, omniscience and omnipresence, but retained his immanent attributes of holiness, love, and truth. But in the main, Kenoticism went far beyond the form of the Logos emptying Himself only of noncommunicable or relative attributes to a denial that in the incarnation any divine attributes remained. But whether in the restricted form or full form Kenoticism is a very serious heresy.

The following is a summary of views of the Kenoticists taken from A. B. Bruce (cited by J. F. Walvoord):

> Fortunately, however, we are not required by the history of opinion to be mathematically complete in our exposition, but may content ourselves with giving some account of four distinct kenotic types, which may for the present be intelligibly, if not felicitously, discriminated as, (1) the absolute dualistic type, (2) the absolute metamorphic, (3) the absolute semi-metamorphic, and (4) the real but relative. Of the first, Thomasius may conveniently be taken as the representative; of the second, Gess; of the third, Ebrard; and of the fourth, Martensen.

J. F. Walvoord describes Bruce's categories as follows, which we quote:

> The first of these described as the absolute dualistic type as set forth. By Thomasius and others attempts to distinguish between the ethical or immanent attributes of God and the relative or physical. According to this view, the relative and physical attributes, including omnipresence, omniscience, and omnipotence, were surrendered by Christ in becoming man. In opposition to this view, orthodox theologians have pointed out that God cannot change his nature by act of his will any more than any other being. Attributes inherent in a personal essence cannot be dismissed. This is contained in the divine attribute of immutability which is expressly affirmed of Christ (Heb

13:8). Further, though there are problems stemming from certain Scriptural statements concerning the human nature of Christ, there is considerable evidence that Christ retained omnipresence, omniscience, and omnipotence even while on earth. Further, a loss in attributes would mean in effect that Christ was not God at all which is contradicted by innumerable Scriptures and specifically by the Gospel of John.

Bruce also points out a second view known as the absolute metamorphic type supported by Gess which goes even further and asserts that divine attributes were given up in the incarnation and Christ was entirely human though Gess asserts according to Bruce that Christ was not "simply an ordinary man," having a "superadamitic element." The divine consciousness in Christ ceased entirely though it was later gradually reassumed, beginning with his experience in the temple at the age of twelve. This point of view is so extreme that it hardly requires refutation by those who accept the Biblical testimony.

The third view, described by Bruce as the "absolute semi-metamorphic type" as espoused by Ebrard is another attempt at compromising the deity of Christ. It held that the divine properties were disguised and appeared as a mode of human existence. The mode of existence of Christ was changed from that of the form of God to the form of a man, from the eternal manner of being to a temporal manner of being. The difficulty with this view is that while it accommodates itself to the human appearance of Christ it in effect denies that He was actually God simultaneously with his human experience. It is not the picture of Christ which is afforded in the entire New Testament.

The fourth view known as the "real but relative" is closer to the truth in that it affirms that Christ was God, but limits his experience to that of the human consciousness and remolds the divine attributes into properties of the human nature. Christ is limited in his experience of knowledge even though as God He was omniscient and limited in his experience of power. This, however, is contradicted by the fact that though Christ in his human nature was limited, his divine consciousness is still omniscient and his divine will still omnipotent. The difficulties with all these views which fall short of ascribing to Christ a full deity is that they read into the passage in Philippians 2 more than it actually says and contradict many other Scriptures which fully assert the deity of Christ during the period He was on earth.

We may now comment on what Walvoord says. The most obvious trouble is that if Christ emptied Himself of even one inherent divine attribute He would no longer be God. Since He is eternal and immutable, God is unable to empty Himself or change his essence in any way. A change would in effect render Him not perfect as He was from all eternity. God the Son did not change in his essence or nature in any way, nor did He empty Himself of any inherent attribute in order to become a man. Christ in his state of humiliation emptied Himself not by the incarnation, but by his own will voluntarily for the purpose of redemption.

Again it is extremely important to distinguish between Christ being emptied of divine attributes themselves and Christ voluntarily laying aside the use of divine attributes that He had during his state of humiliation.

Bickersteth explains it this way, which we quote:

> I think we may safely draw here a parallel betwixt the omnipotence and omniscience of Christ. We have seen that no exception can be taken against his Almighty power as God from the words, "I can of mine own self do nothing." (John 5:30). Because, as man, he wrought his miracles, not by virtue of his Deity, which was ever inherent in him, but by virtue of a perfect faith in the power of the Father (John 14:10), through the plenitude of the Holy Ghost. Though as God ever and always able to do all things, he, of his own Divine will, resolved not to exert this personal omnipotence betwixt his incarnation and his crucifixion. This resolution was part of the act spoken of, Philippians 2:7. We have an illustrious example of this in his thanksgiving prayer, when raising Lazarus from the dead. Father, I thank thee that thou has heard me. And I knew that thou hears me always." (John 11:41-42). So with regard to this other attribute of Deity, omniscience. No exception against his infinite wisdom, as God, can justly be taken from the words, "The Son knows not that day or hour." At his incarnation, he of his own accord resolved not to use, as man, during the days of his humiliation, the knowledge which his omniscience as God would afford. That resolution again was part of act. The wisdom he used was the illumination of the Spirit given to him without measure. The means of its acquirement were diligence and prayer.

> From everlasting to everlasting, before, during, and after his humiliation, Jesus Christ was, and is, and is to come, the Lord God Omnipotent and Omniscient. "Power belongs unto, God," (Psalm 62:11). "Wisdom and might are his," (Daniel 2:20). They are the inalienable attributes of Deity. They could never be laid aside. They could never cease to exist in God. But we must not confound non-existence and non-exertion. Can the Almighty God restrain the use of his power? Indeed so, because the Scripture so declares.

> Thus the patriarch argues, "Will he plead against me with his great power? No," (Job 23:6). Thus the Psalmist records, "He did not stir up all his wrath," (Psalm 78:38). And thus the prophet solaces us, "He stays his rough wind in the day of the cast wind," (Isaiah 27:8). These words indicate that Jehovah did not put forth all his almighty power and all his holy indignation. That is to say, to use the language of men that these attributes were in part unexcited or unexerted. Omnipotence restraining itself is not therefore a view of the acting of

Deity unwarranted by Scripture. Why then should we be stumbled at these expressions of the God-man regarding Himself?

Nay, so far from being staggered at these things, the considerations, which they suggest, are of the utmost value when we contemplate Jesus, as our example. "Who in the days of his flesh offered up prayers and supplications with strong crying and tears to him that was able to save him from death. Who was in all points tempted like as We are; and who in that he has suffered being tempted is able to succor them that are tempted," (Hebrews 2:18; 4:15; 5:7). He put Himself as far as possible on a level with us for "in all things it behooved him to be made like unto his brethren," (Hebrews 2:17). We feel all the persuasive attraction of sympathy. We acknowledge all the power of the example of our elder Brother. We may draw from the same Fountain from whence the man Christ Jesus drew. The way of access through his blood is open to us. The Spirit is willing to strengthen us with might in the inner man. Yea, God in Christ is Himself our wisdom and our strength. We have all the consolations of his perfect humanity; but these truths do not diminish ought from his perfect Divinity. Nay, they glorify it with new beauties, where we see how, in the weakness of human flesh but in the might of Divine faith, how, in the gradual development of human powers but in the full enlightenment of the Divine Spirit, his absolute indefectible goodness, the goodness of infinite love, proved him to be the only-begotten of the Father, God of God, Light of light, very God of very God.

Inferiority of rank as man, as mediator, as the apostle and servant of his Father-having for us spontaneously stooped from the throne of his glory is asserted in the first quotation: equality of nature as to co-operation, self-existence, infinite knowledge, universal trust, is proved in the second.

So wrote Bickersteth.

What it means is that there is no necessity of losing any attributes for the preincarnate Christ to become a true man. We reject the heresy of Kenoticism. In his incarnate state Christ was fully God and only voluntarily refrained from the use of the abilities of attributes that He actually had.

APPENDIX C

COMMUNICABLE ATTRIBUTES AND NATURES

Is what you read here different from what is being taught in most books and tens of thousands of churches and pulpits all over the world? It is without a doubt. Just turn on your radio and you will hear an evangelist preaching Christ as God in all of his divine glory exercising all of his powers, but rarely as the Son of man identifying with us as Jesus did so often when referring to Himself.

It goes without saying that if we do not understand the fundamentals of our Lord's condescension and his humiliation, or if we are confused in the basics of them, our success in fulfilling the great commission and our own sanctification process will be hindered. Satan is a formidable foe and while our victory is guarantied we personally could fall short of our calling and might possibly be the losers. All who are destined to be saved, of course, will be saved and nothing will prevent each of us from entering into his glory, but we can miss our opportunity to fulfill our unique part in the divine process. Without understanding fully the One who is the object of our affections it will be like starting out on a journey without having a definite plan on how to reach the destination. Does being tossed to and fro come to mind? Jesus was a man like you and me, and his example of sanctification should be our daily prompting. Read 2 John 7 - 8 and see how it applies to each of us.

The following, as an exhaustive study on the communicable attributes belongs to some other work. Remember that God says He will not share His glory with another. But what does that mean if we do not understand the attributes that make up that glory? Does He not in fact share his communicable attributes which are some of his glories? It is obvious God will never share his full glory with another, because then at that point He would cease to be the only one who is God.

This is why we need to understand the relationship between God and man. Man is not a god, but has been created in the **image** of God.

We must go into a little detail about what pertains to humanity, or being human. Some attributes of human nature are analogous to attributes of deity. These are commonly called the communicable attributes of God. These human attributes that are analogous to divine attributes are what makes a human being to be in the image of God. Human beings never had and never will have the communicable attributes of God Himself. But they can have attributes analogous to the divine communicable attributes. Actually, it is better to refer to the communicable attributes as analogous attributes, because nothing of divinity is *communicated* to man. The term *image* only indicates something analogous in the creature to the uncreated creator. And what specifically are examples of these communicable attributes? God's communicable attributes include holiness, justice, righteousness, love, mercy, compassion, goodness, benevolence, faithfulness, grace and truth, which may be distinguished from his noncommunicable attributes of omniscience, omnipotence and omnipresence, etc.

And we also need an acceptable meaning for the term *attribute*. The word *attribute* comes to us through the use of logic and is not a term actually used in Scripture. We must define it in such a way as to not violate Scripture. If we cannot do that in a clear way we should simply abandon the term. Connected to the word *attribute* is the word *nature* and that **is** a term used in Scripture. An attribute is something attributed to a person or thing. An attribute may be something inherent to the person or thing but it is not limited to that. It may be something characteristic of persons because of what they do by a voluntary act of will, and therefore not an inherent property of their being. For example, a person may be given to helping others. The fact that they continually **do** this is characteristic of them. But that is not inherent to being human. A person may be charismatic so as to be an excellent leader or even politician, but again that is not inherent to being human. Yet these things are attributes of them.

The word *nature* is also used of God and man. The word *nature* [Greek *phusis*] must be understood in its various contexts. People, animals, plants, and all of creation were made according to its kind and are constant. That is one way in which the term *nature* is used. The word *nature* is not limited in Scripture to referring to species or kind. For instance man is made in the image of God and he never changes from that image. It is his inherent nature. Nevertheless when man sinned we refer to him as having fallen in nature, or that he has a fallen nature. And the consequences of the original sin are passed to all human beings. So men, while they still exist in the image of God, if un-regenerated and remain unbelievers or fallen they are limited to and disposed to act according to their fallen nature. So this is what constitutes a fallen nature. Deeds of the flesh characterize the fallen nature. They are **attributes** of it.

> Gal 5:19 Now the deeds of the flesh are evident, which are:
> immorality, impurity, sensuality, 20 idolatry, sorcery, enmities, strife,
> jealousy, outbursts of anger, disputes, dissensions, factions, 21
> envying, drunkenness, carousing and things like these.

This is one of many lists describing the fallen nature written in Scripture. But just a few verses later Paul lists some of the characteristics of the new nature associated with the divine nature (2 Peter 1:4) created by regeneration by the Holy Spirit when by faith a person repents and commits himself to Christ as Lord.

> Gal 5:22 But the fruit of the Spirit is love, joy, peace, patience,
> kindness, goodness, faithfulness, gentleness, self control.

The first list describes the fallen nature and the latter list belongs to or describes a person in the true uncorrupted image of God, or God's nature. So God is able to change the moral nature of his creature again by regenerating him.

So Scripture teaches that the basic constant or inherent nature of a thing is static as to its creation or its maker's design and does not change kind after kind. But then, on the one hand, it can be perverted, or on the other hand, glorified. It can become enhanced and grow into the full compliment of its original design and fulfill its intended purpose, or else it can become common, debased and rejected from the same original design.

Of course, by sin those analogous attributes in man were corrupted. And the study of the doctrine of man in the study of Systematic Theology goes into that. It is beyond the scope of the book to review that.

We could mention only one other aspect to clarify the word *attribute*. A communicable attribute of God is his attribute of righteousness. But the inherent attribute that makes a person human is obviously not righteousness itself. The analogous attribute in man to the communicable attribute of God is his moral capacity. According to Scripture man is still in the image of God though immoral and not righteous. Theologians refer to what has been dubbed the "covenant of works." Adam was created in righteousness with the attribute of righteousness, but it wasn't completed or perfected. If he had lived out his life in righteousness developed to completion, whatever God determines that is, he would have been **confirmed** in righteousness. The concept of being perfected in righteousness applies to Jesus, because He did what Adam did not do. He lived out his life as Adam should have, and was perfected in righteousness. And because his righteousness is imputed to believers, they become **confirmed** in righteousness.

We may compare Jesus to Adam. Just as Adam was not perfected in the uncorrupted human attributes from the beginning, yet was righteous, etc., so Jesus was not perfected in uncorrupted human attributes from the beginning, though righteous, but became perfected in each analogous or communicable attribute as a man. And as in Adam before the fall, so Jesus during his life was without sin or fault.

The moral attributes of God built into man at the time of his creation are what we are to be perfecting here on earth with whatever time God grants to us. This was Jesus' constant endeavor while obeying the law and fulfilling all righteousness and becoming the perfect representative of man in his original design. Although he was sinless as Adam was, He nevertheless needed to perfect each and every analogous moral attribute of God. He went by his obedience to the Father's will from one level of glory to the next level until all was finished.

END